Also by **Carla Killough McClafferty**

THE HEAD BONE'S CONNECTED TO THE NECK BONE
The Weird, Wacky, and Wonderful X-Ray

Something Out of Nothing

Something Out of Nothing

Marie Curie and Radium

CARLA KILLOUGH McCLAFFERTY

FARRAR STRAUS GIROUX NEW YORK

Designed by Irene Metaxatos
First edition, 2006
Printed in July 2010 in the United States of America
by RR Donnelley & Sons Company, Harrisonburg, Virginia

P1

www.fsgkidsbooks.com

Library of Congress Cataloging-in-Publication Data
McClafferty, Carla Killough, 1958–
    Something out of nothing : Marie Curie and radium / Carla Killough
McClafferty.— 1st ed.
        p.   cm.
    Includes bibliographical references and index.
    ISBN: 978-0-374-37122-7
    1. Curie, Marie, 1867–1934.   2. Radium.   3. Chemists—Poland—Biography.   4. Women
chemists—Poland—Biography.   I. Title.

QD22.C8M25 2006
540'.92—dc22
[B]   2004056414

The author gratefully acknowledges Dr. Graeme M. Luke, Department of Physics and
Astronomy, McMaster University, for his expert reading of the manuscript.

Quotations from MADAME CURIE by Eve Curie, translated by Vincent Sheean, copyright 1937
by Doubleday, a division of Random House, Inc. Used by permission of Doubleday, a division of
Random House, Inc.

Frontispiece: Marie Curie in 1903, the year she won the Nobel Prize in Physics and earned her
doctorate.

For my sisters, Karen McGuire and Debbie Matlock,
who have always been there for me

CONTENTS

A Note to the Reader

When a Polish family name ends in "i," as in Sklodowski, the males in the family use that spelling. However, the females in the family use the feminine form of the name, which ends in "a," as in Sklodowska. The sources I consulted for this book show variations in the spelling of Marie Sklodowska's name. Her nickname is given sometimes as Marya and sometimes as Manya. Her last name is frequently spelled Sklodovska. To be consistent throughout this book, I chose to use Manya Sklodowska.

—CM

Something Out of Nothing

# BEGINNINGS

Warsaw, Poland, 1877

Two long rings, two short—the dreaded warning bell cut through the classroom noise. Four schoolgirls launched into action. Forbidden Polish books and papers were gathered with speed and precision into aprons and hidden. The girls slipped silently back into their seats just before the door opened to reveal the enemy.

Mr. Hornberg, a Russian school inspector, entered the room. He stared through the gold-rimmed glasses perched on his round face at the twenty-five pupils bent over their sewing projects.

He was there to make sure the Polish children, now subjects of the Russian empire, were being taught Russian, and only Russian, history and language. In an attempt to crush the national spirit of the Polish people, it was against the law for them to speak in their native tongue. Even so, Poles kept their language alive both by using it discreetly at home and by secretly teaching it to their children.

Since being divided between Prussia, Austria, and Russia in the late 1700s, Poland had been erased from the maps of the world. It existed only in the hearts of its people.

Inspector Hornberg squeezed into a chair and said to the teacher, "Please call on one of these young people."

Ten-year-old Marie Salomée Sklodowska, the youngest pupil in the class, whispered a silent prayer that *for once* the teacher would not pick on her. Marie was usually chosen to answer the inspector's questions because of her incredible memory. Everyone knew she could recite a poem by heart after reading it twice.

"Manya Sklodowska," the teacher called out, using her nickname.

At the sound of her name, a familiar dread washed over her. Shivers of fear ran down her spine. She wanted to run and hide every time she had to speak before the class. But there was nowhere to go.

Manya sat up straighter in her chair, smoothed down her navy blue uniform, and waited.

"Your prayer," Inspector Hornberg ordered.

Past the lump in her throat, Manya spoke with a perfect Russian accent. "Our Father, Which art in heaven, hallowed be Thy name . . ."

Inspector Hornberg asked question after question about the tsars and imperial families of Russia. Manya answered each one correctly.

Then he asked one final question to remind them who was in charge: "Who rules over us?"

Manya hesitated, the lump in her throat getting bigger.

"Who rules over us?" he demanded, louder this time.

She forced the answer he wanted from her lips, in Russian: "His Majesty Alexander II, Tsar of all the Russias."

Satisfied with her answer, Inspector Hornberg rose from his chair and with a brief nod left the room.

Once again Manya had done her duty.

The Polish teacher called out to her smallest student with the long blond braids, "Come here, my little soul."

Manya went to her. Her teacher kissed her on the forehead. Manya burst into tears.

Stage fright was a small thing compared to the problems Manya Sklodowska had already experienced in her short life. Ever since Manya's birth on November 7, 1867, her mother had been sick. Bronislawa Sklodowska had tuberculosis. To help prevent her family from catching the disease, she kept the dishes she used apart from the others. And for the safety of her children, of whom Manya was the youngest, she'd decided never to hug or kiss them. Instead of kissing, her mother had always shown affection by running her fingertips lightly over Manya's forehead.

Mrs. Sklodowska cared for her family and pretended she wasn't as sick as she really was. She used the little energy she had to make leather shoes at home for her five children. Although she tried to hide it from them, the family could hear her frequent dry coughing coming from another room of the house.

By 1873, not only was Manya's mother ill, but her father, Vladislav Sklodowski, had problems at work. As a professor of mathematics and physics and an under-inspector at a boys' secondary school, he had the difficult task of teaching his Polish students while trying to satisfy Principal Ivanov, his Russian boss.

Ivanov disliked Mr. Sklodowski and accused him of not being pro-Russian enough. He arranged to have Mr. Sklodowski's job of under-

The five Sklodowski children all had nicknames. Pictured here from left to right are Sophia (Zosia), Helena (Hela), Marie (Manya), Joseph (Jozio), and Bronislawa (Bronya).

inspector taken away from him. This meant that his salary was reduced, and the nice house where the family had been living for free was taken away from them.

The Sklodowski family had no choice but to move into an apartment. To bring in extra money, the family took in boarders so that Manya's father could tutor them. As many as ten boys at a time lived with them temporarily, crowding their small apartment.

Then death entered the Sklodowski home. In January 1876, one of the boarders brought more than books when he came to stay. He was a carrier of typhus, a deadly disease that can be spread by contaminated lice. Two of Manya's sisters, Bronislawa and Sophia, caught the disease. Bronislawa (Bronya for short) slowly recovered from the high fever, but fourteen-year-old Sophia died.

Mrs. Sklodowska, too weak from tuberculosis to leave the house and accompany her family to the Catholic funeral, watched from the window as her daughter's coffin was carried down the street. Eight-year-old Manya joined the other mourners as they made their way to the cemetery.

This was the first coffin Manya would follow. And it would not be the last.

Mrs. Sklodowska's condition worsened, despite the family's evening prayers to "restore our mother's health." Manya went to church each day to pray that her faithful mother's life might be spared. With gray eyes like her once-beautiful mother's, Manya watched as her mother grew thinner and weaker from the fever and bloody cough.

On May 9, 1878, Manya's mother died.

Her beloved mother's death made a lasting impact on ten-year-old Manya. Many years later she wrote that it "threw me into a profound depression." Although she continued to go to church with her family as she had done before, something had changed for Manya. Deep inside she rejected the faith her mother had cherished. For the rest of her life she never maintained any kind of religious belief.

Manya, who had been reading since she was four years old, escaped the sorrow of her mother's death by focusing her attention on books of all kinds: poetry, adventure stories, even her father's physics journals.

When the children gathered each evening around the big table to study, Manya got into position so she could concentrate. She put her elbows on the table, head in her hands, and thumbs in her ears. In that way she could ignore all the noise and activity in the room and totally direct her attention to her homework.

On one occasion, her sisters Bronya and Hela decided to see just how well Manya could ignore everything going on around her. While Manya sat motionless in her position, the girls built a pyramid of chairs beside her and over her head. She didn't even realize this was happening. Her sisters sat down to wait and see how long it would take Manya to notice. They giggled and waited. And waited and giggled. About thirty minutes later, Manya closed her book and lifted her head. When she did, an avalanche of chairs fell to the floor. Bronya and Hela howled with laughter.

"That's stupid!" said Manya in her usual serious tone as she pushed past the practical jokers.

When Manya was fourteen, it was time to leave behind her old school where Polish teachers had secretly taught in Polish. Now she would attend a school where all the teachers were Russian.

Fourteen-year-old Manya as she looked during her last year of high school. By that time she could speak Polish, Russian, French, German, and English.

The Russian teachers treated their Polish students like enemies. Manya and her friends understood they must watch every word they said. They must not speak Polish when they could be overheard by someone, because a police informant might be listening.

Many years later, Manya described what this was like.

Constantly held in suspicion and spied upon, the children knew that a single conversation in Polish, or an imprudent word, might seriously harm, not only themselves, but also their families. Amidst these hostilities, they lost all the joy of life, and precocious feelings of distrust and indignation weighed upon their childhood. On the other side, this abnormal situation resulted in exciting the patriotic feeling of Polish youths to the highest degree.

The Russian authorities were always on their guard for hints of rebellion from the Poles. Any kind of trouble was dealt with harshly. When Manya was fifteen, the danger of defying the Russians hit close to home.

At dance class one day, Léonie Kunicka, a friend of Manya's, arrived in tears. When Manya and Kazia Przyborovska, her best friend, raced toward her to see what was wrong, Léonie said, "It's my brother . . . He was in a plot . . . He was denounced . . . We haven't known where he was for three days . . . They are going to hang him tomorrow."

Manya and her sisters Bronya and Hela, and Kazia and her sister Ula, stayed with Léonie throughout the night. Their hearts were full of anger and their eyes full of tears as dawn approached.

At the break of day, Léonie Kunicka's brother was executed.

The authorities might govern the actions of Poles, but they could never govern their hearts. As Manya and Kazia walked to school, they passed by a town square in Warsaw. The Russian government had erected a monument there to honor Polish people who had made friends with the Russians. The inscription read, "To the Poles faithful to their Sovereign." Manya and Kazia believed these people were traitors to Poland. Each day when they walked past the monument, Manya and Kazia spit on the ground. If by chance they were busy talking and forgot, they made a point of walking by again so they could continue their symbolic revolution.

Manya was first in her class when she graduated from secondary school at fifteen. Like her brother, Joseph, and sister Bronya before her, she was awarded a gold medal for her accomplishments. Manya worked so hard at her studies that after graduation she was physically and emotionally exhausted. It isn't clear exactly what Manya's problems were, but her family called them "nervous troubles." Years later she wrote, "The fatigue of growth and study compelled me to take almost a year's rest in the country."

To recover her health, her father sent Manya to southern Poland to stay by turns with her various uncles and their families. Manya, accompanied by Lancet, the family's large brown dog, went from place to place, sometimes as far south as the Carpathian Mountains.

During her vacation, Manya developed a deep love for nature as she roamed through the woods and swam in the river. She dedicated herself as much to having fun as she had to studying. When she returned to Warsaw in the summer of 1884, she brought back many sweet memories.

It was time to put her vacation aside and get a job to help support the family. To do so, Manya privately taught the children of wealthy people. This was the only respectable job in those times for a young woman who was poor but well educated.

But Manya dreamed of more.

GOVERNESS

Hela pursued a teaching career while Manya and Bronya both wanted to study at a university like their brother, Joseph. Women in Poland were not allowed to attend college in their own country but were not prevented from being educated elsewhere. Coming from a family who shared a deep desire for learning, the sisters looked for ways to continue their studies. For the time being, they attended what was called the "Floating University," a secret school taught by Polish scientists, philosophers, and historians of literature and culture. Classes for up to ten people were held in different homes. Participation was dangerous. If discovered, both students and teachers could be sent to prison. For about a year, Manya and Bronya studied anatomy, natural history, and sociology through this underground network.

But their greatest dream was to attend the University of Paris, known as the Sorbonne. The young women had to begin saving money if there was to be any chance of getting there.

Bronya, already twenty years old, wanted to become a doctor but had only enough savings for one year of school in Paris.

Manya came up with a plan. They could help each other. She suggested that Bronya use the money she'd already saved and go to the Sorbonne in the coming year. Meanwhile, seventeen-year-old Manya would get a full-time job as a governess and send Bronya most of her earnings. Manya's money, in addition to the little bit their father could add, would be enough to support Bronya in Paris as she got her education. Then, when Bronya became a doctor, she could in turn help Manya through school.

Bronya resisted the idea. How could she go when it meant leaving her sister to work and support her for years before Manya had a chance to go herself?

Yet no matter how many times they tried to find another way, Manya's plan seemed the only possibility.

So Bronya headed for the Sorbonne, and Manya found a job as a governess for a wealthy family in Warsaw. She didn't like the family or the way they treated her. On December 10, 1885, in a letter to her cousin Henrietta Michalovska, Manya wrote, "My existence has been that of a prisoner . . . In the end, my relations with Mme B— had become so icy that I could not endure it any longer and told her so."

She also found that even though she still lived with her father in Warsaw, her salary did not allow her to save enough money to send to Bronya. Manya needed to find a governess job that paid more.

A family named Zorawski offered her a job for a larger salary plus free room and board. The only problem was that they lived in Szczuki, a small village away from Warsaw. Manya didn't want to live so far from home and her father, but she'd made a commitment to Bronya.

Manya accepted the job. She consoled herself that at least she loved being in the country.

She was eighteen years old when she traveled to Szczuki to live and work as a governess with the family she had not yet even met. Manya wrote, "My heart was heavy as I climbed into the railway car. It was to carry me for several hours, away from those I loved. And after the railway journey I must drive for five hours longer. What experience was awaiting me?"

Fortunately, Manya liked the Zorawskis. Her job was to teach two daughters of the family, one of whom was her own age. The family had other children as well: two sons were away at boarding school in Warsaw and another attended the university there. They also had a three-year-old son and a six-month-old daughter.

In February 1886, Manya described her charges in a letter to her cousin Henrietta: "I have made friends with their eldest daughter, Bronka, which contributes to the pleasantness of my life. As for my pupil Andzia, who will soon be ten, she is an obedient child, but very disorderly and spoiled. Still, one can't require perfection."

Although her work kept her busy, after becoming acquainted with the village she realized that few local children had ever been to school and that they had learned only the Russian alphabet. With the approval of her employers, she taught the village children to read and write in Polish. She would help her country by educating its less privileged. Manya understood the risks and cautioned the family that "even this innocent work present[s] danger, as all initiative of this kind [is] forbidden by the government and might bring imprisonment or deportation to Siberia."

Manya not only taught others during this time but continued studying herself. She was interested in literature, sociology, science, and mathematics and tried to decide what to concentrate on when her turn would come to go to the university. Eventually she set her mind to study math and physics. She knew the scientific education she'd received was inferior to courses taught in French schools. Since she had no access to a teacher, her father helped her improve her math skills through their letters to each other. She pored over any science textbook she could get her hands on. She described her study habits in a letter to Henrietta: "At nine in the evening I take my books and go to work, if something unexpected does not prevent it . . . I have even acquired the habit of getting up at six so that I work more." Many years later, Manya recalled this as a time when she "acquired the habit of independent work, and learned a few things which were to be of use later on."

Then everything changed.

Casimir Zorawski, the family's eldest son, came home from the university on vacation. He thought Manya was beautiful, with her curly blond hair and expressive gray eyes. Casimir liked that she was different from other girls he knew. Not only was Manya intelligent and witty, she enjoyed activities such as riding horses, skating, and dancing.

Manya and Casimir fell in love and made plans to marry. Casimir knew his parents liked Manya and was sure they would be delighted at the prospect. As was expected in those days, he went to his parents to ask their approval for the marriage.

Their reaction shocked him. His father was furious and his mother nearly fainted when she heard. Their answer was clear: he could not marry Manya.

They explained to their son that they liked and respected Manya. She was from a good family. But she was poor. The son of an aristocratic family must not marry the governess, no matter how appealing she was. His parents assured Casimir that, as a wealthy young man, he could have his pick of any wealthy young woman.

Casimir obeyed his parents. He told Manya there would be no marriage.

Manya was heartbroken. How could she stay there knowing they thought she wasn't good enough to marry their son? The family had always treated her as a friend, but now . . . Manya wanted to leave, to get away from these people who had pretended to accept her as an equal.

But Bronya needed half of Manya's paycheck to be able to stay in school in Paris. Manya knew from her previous job search that no one paid more for a governess than the Zorawski family.

And so she stayed with the family that rejected her.

Manya never discussed the situation with Casimir's parents, her employers. She continued her routine through a haze of misery, teaching the Zorawski children and the village children and studying on her own. The warmth she'd once felt toward the Zorawski family was gone. And when Casimir came home on vacation, she had to endure seeing the one who had broken her heart.

A deep depression settled upon eighteen-year-old Manya. A letter to Henrietta in December 1886 seems to suggest she even thought of suicide:

My plans for the future? I have none, or rather they are so commonplace and simple that they are not worth talking about. I mean to get through as well as

I can, and when I can do no more, say farewell to this base world. The loss will be small, and regret for me will be short—as short as for so many others.

These are my only plans now. Some people pretend that in spite of everything I am obliged to pass through the kind of fever called love. This absolutely does not enter into my plans. If I ever had any others, they have gone up in smoke; I have buried them; locked them up; sealed and forgotten them.

Rejection ripped away Manya's self-confidence and replaced it with doubt about herself and her future. In a letter to her brother, Joseph, in March 1887, she wrote: "now that I have lost the hope of ever becoming anybody, all my ambition has been transferred to Bronya and you." Two months later she confessed in another letter to him that she was "afraid for myself: it seems to me all the time that I am getting terribly stupid—the days pass so quickly and I make no noticeable progress."

She hid her broken heart from the Zorawski family as the next year crept by. Everything had changed, but everyone pretended it hadn't. The only thing that stayed the same was the money she sent each month to Bronya.

She poured out her continued turmoil in a letter to Joseph in March 1888:

If you only knew how I sigh and long to go to Warsaw for only a few days! I say nothing of my clothes, which are worn out and need care—but my soul, too, is worn out. Ah, if I could extract myself for just a few days from this icy atmosphere of criticism, from the perpetual guard over my own words, the expression in my face, my gestures! . . . . If I only didn't have to think of Bronya I should present my resignation to the Z.'s this very instant and look for another post, even though this one is so well paid.

Then, more than two years after her arrival, things began to change for the better for Manya. In April, her father retired from his old teaching job and took a different position as director of a reform school. The work was difficult but the pay was good, so he was able to help Bronya more than before. Bronya insisted that Manya stop sending her money and that their father take part of what he was sending Bronya and save it for Manya's education.

For the first time since she went to work, Manya was saving money for her own education.

Toward the end of 1888, Manya knew she was almost finished educating the Zorawskis' daughters. In less than a year, she would leave them. In November 1888, she wrote Henrietta:

Everybody says that I have changed a great deal, physically and spiritually, during my stay at Szczuki. This is not surprising. I was barely eighteen when I came here, and what have I not been through! There have been moments which I shall certainly count among the most cruel of my life . . . and it seems to me that I am coming out of a nightmare . . . First principle: never to let one's self be beaten down by persons or by events.

Manya left the Zorawski family in June 1889, after three years in their home. She wanted to forget those who had caused her such pain. When she returned to Warsaw, she accepted another job as a governess.

By March 1890, Bronya had only one more year left of school before she completed her studies to become a gynecologist. She had meanwhile fallen in love with Casimir Dluski, a Polish doctor whom she planned to marry. Bronya wrote Manya, "And now you, my little Manya: you must make something of your life sometime . . . come to Paris next year and live with us, where you will find board and lodging."

Manya wrote back, "I have been stupid, I am stupid and I shall remain stupid all the days of my life . . . I have never been, am not and shall never be lucky. I dreamed of Paris as of redemption, but the hope of going there left me a long time ago."

Bronya insisted. Finally, Manya folded under her sister's pressure and agreed to make the trip. But she couldn't go right away. First she had to complete her one-year commitment as gover-ness. Then she wanted to spend a year with her father, who had retired from his job.

During the time in her father's home, Manya tutored students and once again participated in the Floating University. She attended secretly held classes at the Museum of Industry and Agriculture, which included a small laboratory. Her cousin Joseph Boguski, who had been an assistant in Rus-sia to the well-known chemist Dmitri Mendeleev, was the museum's director. Boguski's "museum" ti-tle was meant to mislead Russian authorities; the museum's real purpose was to teach science to Pol-ish students involved with the Floating University.

Manya in 1888, during her last year working as a governess for the Zorawski family. It was a time of unhappiness and self-doubt for her.

Manya was introduced to laboratory work for the first time in her life. Her only free time to work in the lab was after dinner and on Sundays, which meant she was often there alone.

Years later Manya would describe her initial experience in this laboratory:

To my great joy, I was able, for the first time in my life, to find access to a laboratory . . . At times I would be encouraged by a little unhoped-for success, at others I would be in the deepest despair because of accidents and failures resulting from my inexperience. But on the whole, though I was taught that the way of progress is neither swift nor easy, this first trial confirmed in me the taste for experimental research in the fields of physics and chemistry.

By September 1891, Manya was ready for the next phase of her life, but only after she'd met with Casimir Zorawski one last time and it became clear that he would never marry her against the wishes of his family. She wrote Bronya, "I ask you for a definite answer. Decide if you can really take me in at your house, for I can come now."

For Bronya it was an easy decision. She wanted Manya to arrive in time to begin classes in November.

Four weeks later, Manya was packed and ready to leave for Paris.

Household items such as her mattress, sheets, and towels were shipped ahead so Manya wouldn't have to purchase them in Paris at a higher price. She bought a fourth-class train ticket, the cheapest way to travel to France. Traveling fourth class meant she took her own folding chair to sit in the middle of a railcar lined around the edges with benches. And she took enough food and drink from home to last the three-day trip.

Manya assured her father when she said goodbye that she would "not be away long . . . two years, three at the longest. As soon as I have finished my studies, and passed a few examinations, I'll come back, and we shall live together and never be separated again."

It had been eight years since she'd graduated at the top of her high school class. At last, Manya was going to college.

PIERRE

Freedom.

Manya was free for the first time in her life. She could go wherever she wanted without wondering if someone was watching. She was free to speak Polish without fear that someone might be listening. She could read Polish books in public if she wanted, and nobody cared. She was free from the responsibility of being a governess for the first time in years.

Everything in the centuries-old city of Paris was new to Manya: the Eiffel Tower, which had recently been built; the beautiful bridges that

Twenty-four-year-old Marie standing on the balcony of Bronya's home in Paris, 1892. She had been at the Sorbonne for only a few months when this photo was taken.

arched gracefully over the river Seine; the towers and spires of Notre Dame, which rose from a tiny island in the middle of the swirling river; even the Louvre, which had been a public museum for almost one hundred years. She would later write, "All that I saw and learned that was new delighted me. It was like a new world opened to me."

As planned, Manya moved in with Bronya and her husband, Casimir Dluski.

When Manya registered at the Sorbonne in late October 1891, she left behind her family's nickname for her. From this point on, she would be known as Marie.

Bronya and Casimir's home was a riot of activity. Since they were both doctors, an almost constant stream of patients came to their home office at odd hours. And their doors were always open to friends who counted on fun-loving Casimir to keep them entertained.

So much was going on around Marie in their home that it was hard for her to concentrate on her studies. She realized she needed to catch up in some areas of physics and math to compete with her French classmates. Although her French was already good, she worked on it until she spoke it perfectly, with only a trace of a rolled "r" left from her native language.

Marie enjoyed living with the Dluskis and liked her brother-in-law. But she said he "had the habit of disturbing me endlessly. He absolutely could not endure having me do anything but engage in agreeable chatter with him when I was at home." And Marie wanted to study.

Their apartment on the northern outskirts of Paris was a long way from the Sorbonne. Each day Marie paid the fare for the horse-drawn bus to take her back and forth to school—an hour's trip each way. The expense cut into Marie's small savings and took away a lot of study time.

After a few months of living with Bronya and Casimir, Marie decided to move closer to the university.

In March 1892, she rented the first of several cheap rooms she would live in during her years as a student. They were all located near the Sorbonne in a section of the city known as the Latin Quarter, where mostly students and artists lived. She could have found a roommate but chose to live by herself, even though it meant a heavier financial burden. One of her early apartments was more like an attic room. It was on the sixth floor and had no electric light or heat. Her only water supply was a faucet on the stair landing. Marie later wrote, "It was not unusual for the water to freeze in the basin in the night; to be able to sleep I was obliged to pile all my clothes on the bedcovers." On especially cold nights, in an effort to feel a bit warmer, she would put the only chair in her room on top of the bedcovers to weigh them down.

Marie would study at the school library until it closed each night at ten o'clock. As she walked alone through the streets of Paris toward her apartment, she'd pass the Pantheon, the building where Jean-Bernard-Léon Foucault had used a pendulum to prove the earth spins on its axis, and where some of France's famous dead were buried. After she arrived at her apartment, she would study by lamplight until two in the morning.

To stretch her funds, Marie ate as little as possible. Her meals "were often reduced to bread with a cup of chocolate, eggs or fruit."

Marie's habit of studying too much and not eating enough caught up with her one day when she fainted on the sidewalk in front of her apartment building. A friend who saw what happened reported it to Casimir and Bronya. Casimir raced to Marie's apartment, where he found her studying as usual. Looking around her room, he saw no food and only one package of tea. He was able to get Marie to confess that she'd slept no more than four hours the previous night, and that a few radishes and a half pound of cherries were all she'd eaten that day.

Ignoring her protests, Casimir forced Marie to accompany him home to Bronya, who fed and cared for her. But after just a few days of nutrition and rest, Marie went back to her apartment and her old way of life. Ever afterward Casimir jokingly called this "the heroic period of my sister-in-law's life."

Despite the difficulties, Marie enjoyed being a student:

It would be impossible to tell of all the good these years brought to me. Undistracted by any outside occupation, I was entirely absorbed in the joy of learning and understanding . . . This life, painful from certain points of view, had, for all that, a real charm for me. It gave me a very precious sense of liberty and independence . . . I shall always consider one of the best memories of my life that period of solitary years exclusively devoted to the studies, finally within my reach, for which I had waited so long.

Her years of study paid off when she gradated first in her class in 1893. Marie Sklodowska was the first woman to receive a master's degree in physics from the Sorbonne. But she wasn't satisfied. She also wanted a degree in math.

After graduation she gave up her apartment, stored her meager possessions with a classmate, and returned to Poland. Even as she enjoyed being home with her father, she worried about going back to school in the fall. Her savings were nearly gone.

Fortunately, a friend of Marie's in Warsaw helped her obtain the Alexandrovitch Scholarship, given to gifted Polish students who wanted to study abroad. The scholarship money would allow Marie to live on in Paris for fifteen months, long enough for her to earn her second master's degree.

When she returned to Paris, she rented a better apartment than the ones she'd had the previous years. She wrote her brother, Joseph, on September 15, 1893, that she was "very satisfied with this room: it has a window that shuts tight, and when I have arranged it properly it should not be cold here, especially as the floor is of wood and not tiles. Compared to my last year's room it is a veritable palace."

In addition to her classes, Marie had a job. She had been hired by the Society for the Encouragement of National Industry, a public company dedicated to developing and promoting French products of all kinds. The society wanted her to initiate long-term research study on the magnetic properties of various types of steel.

By the beginning of 1894, Marie started her work on steel at the Sorbonne in the laboratory of Professor Gabriel Lippmann (who would in 1908 be awarded a Nobel Prize in Physics for his contribution to the advancement of color photography). But she realized she would need a larger area in which to work.

During a trip to Paris in the spring of 1894, a Polish scientist named Joseph Kowalski and his wife, who knew Marie from her governess days, visited her. As their conversation turned toward their work, Marie mentioned her need for more laboratory space. Kowalski said he knew a scientist in the city who was a professor at the School of Physics and Chemistry and suggested that he might have a room Marie could use. Kowalski invited both Marie and this scientist to tea the next evening.

It was a meeting that would change Marie's life. The scientist's name was Pierre Curie.

Marie described the first time she saw Pierre:

Upon entering the room I perceived, standing framed by the French window opening on the balcony, a tall young man with auburn hair and large, limpid eyes. I noticed the grave and gentle expression of his face, as well as a certain abandon in his attitude, suggesting the dreamer absorbed in his reflections.

Unfortunately, Pierre could not offer Marie any help with lab space. He had the same problem and was conducting his own research on various types of magnetism in the hallway outside his classroom.

Pierre Curie had earned a bachelor's degree in science at the age of sixteen and a master's degree in physics at eighteen. At nineteen he had gone to work as a laboratory assistant and begun his research career.

He was thirty-five years old when he met Marie and was already a well-known scientist. Pierre and his brother, Jacques, had discovered piezoelectricity through their work on crystals. Piezoelectricity is the tiny amount of electricity that is produced when pressure is applied to certain crystals. Their research was instrumental in the development of various products that use piezoelectricity today, such as quartz crystal watches, radio transmitters, radar devices, phonograph needles, and microphones. Next the Curie brothers invented the piezoelectric quartz electrometer, an instrument capable of precisely measuring small amounts of electric current.

Pierre Curie was completely absorbed in his work and never expected to meet someone like Marie. At twenty-six, she was beautiful and smart— and understood him when he talked about his scientific work.

As they got to know each other during the spring of 1894, they realized they had much in common. They both held a deep love for their families and nature, and both made science their religion. By early summer 1894, Marie had graduated second in her class with a master's degree in math and Pierre had asked her to marry him. He wanted her to share his "dream of an existence consecrated entirely to scientific research."

Marie was torn over what to do. She wanted to come back to Paris to earn a doctorate, but she also wanted to return to Russian-controlled Poland to help her countrymen by educating them. Also, she had promised her father that she would come back and live with him again.

Marie did not accept Pierre's marriage proposal. When she left, they parted with the promise that they would always have a "great affection" for each other.

Once back in Warsaw, Marie was unsure whether she would return to Paris, despite her desire for a doctorate.

Meanwhile, Pierre began a letter-writing campaign to convince Marie to come back. Although he wanted most of all for her to reconsider and marry him, he tried to appeal to her longing to live a life devoted to scientific research. He understood her wish to help educate Poland's people, but he wanted to convince her that this alone could not change the political oppression there. He did, however, believe that they could make the world a better place through science. On August 10, 1894, he wrote:

It would, nevertheless, be a beautiful thing in which I hardly dare believe, to pass through life together hypnotized in our dreams: your dream for your

country; our dream for humanity; our dream for science. Of all these dreams,
I believe the last, alone, is legitimate. I mean to say by this that we are pow-
erless to change the social order.

And on September 7:

I shall be very unhappy if you do not come this year . . . I believe you will
work better here and that you can accomplish here something more substan-
tial and more useful.

By the middle of September, Marie decided to return to Paris to finish
the study on steel she'd been doing and to work toward her doctorate at
the Sorbonne. This time she lived for free in a room that adjoined Bronya's
medical office.

Pierre was in love with Marie and continually tried to convince her to
marry him. He even offered to move to Poland with her, if that was what
she wanted. But Marie would not allow Pierre to leave the freedom of
France to go to her oppressed homeland. On the other hand, how could
she marry Pierre and live freely in Paris when she could be helping her
countrymen?

What should she do?

She would marry Pierre. An 1895 letter from her brother dated
July 14—the French national holiday, Bastille Day—must have been a re-
lief to her.

I think you are right to follow your heart, and no just person can reproach
you for it. Knowing you, I am convinced that you will remain Polish with all
your soul . . . I would infinitely rather see you in Paris, happy and contented,

than back again in our country, broken by the sacrifice of a whole life and victim of a too-subtle conception of your duty.

Marie wrote her childhood friend Kazia:

When you receive this letter your Manya will have changed her name. I am about to marry the man I told you about last year in Warsaw. It is a sorrow to me to have to stay forever in Paris, but what am I to do? Fate has made us deeply attached to each other and we cannot endure the idea of separating . . . Finally I became reconciled to the idea of settling here. When you receive this letter, write to me: Madame Curie, School of Physics and Chemistry, 42 Rue Lhomond. That is my name from now on.

Marie married Pierre Curie on July 26, 1895, about four months after he had earned his doctorate. Since neither wanted any type of religious ceremony, they were wed at the city hall of Sceaux, the small town near Paris where Pierre still lived with his parents. Only their families and a few close friends of Pierre's were invited. Marie insisted that her wedding dress be dark and practical so she could wear it to work later in the laboratory. They didn't even exchange wedding rings.

The newlyweds settled into their first apartment with only a vase of flowers and the bare necessities: a bed, a table, two chairs, and a lamp. They didn't plan to have many visitors, so they didn't have a sofa or an extra chair. Marie had never been interested in cooking, cleaning, or home decorating. She preferred bare floors and walls, along with curtainless windows, and that was how the apartment would be.

Now that she was married, Marie decided she needed cooking lessons.

She asked Mrs. Dluski, Bronya's mother-in-law, to teach her. Marie approached cooking as if it were a scientific experiment. She made careful notes in the margins of her cookbooks about the successes and failures of her attempts.

The Curies built their lives around scientific research, as they'd planned. Pierre studied crystals and Marie continued her study of the magnetic qualities of steel. Pierre's boss allowed Marie to share research space with Pierre at the School of Physics and Chemistry, where he was a professor. They walked arm in arm to their laboratory and back every day.

While Marie and Pierre were absorbed in each other and their work, other scientists were making incredible discoveries. In November 1895, Dr. Wilhelm Conrad Roentgen, a German physicist, discovered the X-ray, a type of electromagnetic radiation that has a very short wavelength and can penetrate most objects. The power of the invisible rays caused many scientists to question if there were other forms of radiation (the energy transported by rays or waves or particles) that hadn't been discovered yet.

As soon as Dr. Henri Becquerel, a scientist in Paris, heard about the dis-

With money they received as a wedding gift, the Curies bought two new bicycles. The newlyweds spent the first couple of weeks of their honeymoon pedaling through France, enjoying the sights of the countryside, and stopping along the way to eat picnic lunches of bread, cheese, and fruit. At the end of the day, they would stay in a country inn.

covery of X-rays, he wondered if fluorescent substances might produce them. Fluorescent substances emit light when exposed to electromagnetic radiation such as sunshine.

To test his theory, he placed various samples, one at a time, on glass photographic plates covered with black paper. The paper protected the plates from light but would not prevent X-rays from passing through them. Then he placed each test set in the sunlight for a while. Next he developed the photographic plates to see if there was any X-ray exposure on them. When he found no image on the developed plate, it meant that the sample he tested did not emit X-rays even when it fluoresced.

Near the end of February 1896, Becquerel prepared his experiment using a sample containing the element uranium. (An element is a fundamental substance that cannot be broken down chemically any further.) But it was a cloudy day, so he put the uranium sample and plate in a drawer to await the next sunny day. On March 1, he took it out and developed the photographic plate, and to his surprise, an image appeared on the plate. Somehow the uranium had emitted radiation even without exposure to sunlight. News of Becquerel's uranium rays spread through the scientific community.

Marie was fascinated by uranium rays and studied Dr. Becquerel's publication about them. As a scientist, she wondered what caused the uranium sample to spontaneously emit radiation. Her thoughts returned to the mystery again and again.

In 1897, after three years' work, Marie successfully completed her research on the magnetic properties of steel and was paid in full. She used some of her earnings to repay the money she'd received from the Alexandrovitch Scholarship. She didn't have to do so—the money had been a gift. But Marie remembered that without the scholarship she would not have

been able to earn her master's degree in math. She believed that if she returned the money, she could help another Polish student like herself. It
was a way to give something back to Poland.

As Marie's work project came to an end, a personal project was just beginning. On September 12, 1897, her daughter Irène was born.

Although it was unusual for the times in which they lived, neither Marie
nor Pierre considered that Marie should give up her scientific career to
stay home with Irène. Pierre's father, Eugène Curie, a retired doctor whose
wife had recently died, agreed to live with them and care for Irène while
Marie worked at the laboratory.

With Dr. Curie settled in as baby-sitter for Irène, Marie turned her
thoughts to her next goal—her doctorate. She needed to determine the
topic of her doctoral thesis, a report written on original research. Marie
chose Dr. Becquerel's uranium rays. The subject had not been studied in
depth by another scientist, which meant the research would require hands-
on work rather than mostly library research. It was perfect for Marie, who
was happiest in a laboratory.

Once again, Marie needed a place where she could conduct her research. Pierre's boss at the School of Physics and Chemistry agreed to let
her use the only space available, located on Rue Lhomond—Lhomond
Street. But it wasn't much—an old glassed-in shed that had previously
been used as a storeroom.

Even so, the work of a lifetime was about to begin.

DISCOVERY

The shed offered little protection from the winter's cold as Marie began her study of uranium rays. On February 6, 1898, she recorded in her notebook the temperature inside her shed: forty-three degrees Fahrenheit. Ignoring the cold, she set out to learn everything she could about Dr. Becquerel's rays. Starting only with the knowledge that uranium spontaneously produced radiation, she sought to determine how much radiation her uranium sample produced.

Marie knew from the work of Roentgen and

Becquerel that when radiation was present, the air around the sample became a conductor of electricity. Therefore she could measure the amount of radiation from each sample by the amount of electricity the air conducted. She needed a precise instrument capable of detecting tiny amounts of electricity. Fortunately, Pierre and Jacques had already developed the piezoelectric quartz electrometer, which was perfect for the job.

As Marie continued her study of uranium rays, she became convinced that the radiation came from the uranium's atoms. (An atom is the smallest component of an element.) She wondered if any other elements besides

Inside the shed where Marie began her work that led to the discovery of radium. The shed was hot in the summer and freezing in winter, and rain plopped down on the Curies' equipment all year long. Eventually, everything in the lab became radioactive, including notebooks, clothes, walls, furniture, and even the air.

uranium emitted radiation. After testing with the electrometer all the elements known to the scientific world at the time, she found that thorium also emitted radiation. The ability of these two elements—uranium and thorium—to produce radiation spontaneously was completely new to science. Since there wasn't even a word to describe this phenomenon, she created one: *radioactivité*. In English it's almost exactly the same: *radioactivity*.

Marie borrowed metal, mineral, salt, and oxide samples from various scientists and tested each one. Samples that were radioactive she studied further. In some, she noticed that the amount of radiation emitted was higher than it should have been, considering the amount of uranium and thorium they contained. At first she thought she must have made a mistake in the evaluation process. But she tested the samples over and over, and each time the result was the same. Since the samples emitted far more radiation than either of the two known radioactive elements could have made possible, she suspected she'd found a new element. Marie confided to Bronya, "The radiation that I couldn't explain comes from a new chemical element. The element is there and I've got to find it."

Pierre was fascinated by the possibility that Marie could have made such a discovery. Around June 1898, they decided that Pierre would temporarily set aside his study of crystals and join Marie in search of this unknown element. They knew it would be difficult but believed that together they would get faster results.

From the moment Pierre joined Marie in her project, they became a perfect lab team. They worked together almost as if they were one person instead of two, with each of their handwritten notes alternating at times on the same page. Scientific papers written by either of them say "we" did this or "we" did that. If they made a reference to an experiment accomplished by only one of them, they wrote "one of us" without naming which one.

Pages from a notebook used by Marie and Pierre in 1898. The handwriting of both fills the pages, demonstrating their teamwork. Notebooks used in their lab are still radioactive. To view them at the Bibliothèque Nationale, the national library of France, a researcher must sign a form releasing the library from responsibility for any "possible risks of radioactivity."

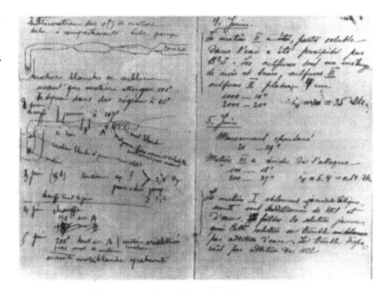

In Marie's research she found that pitchblende, a black or brown mineral containing uranium and lead, among other things, was about four times more radioactive than uranium. She therefore concentrated her study on pitchblende. Using chemical analysis, she and Pierre broke down the pitchblende and took out all the known components, leaving only the parts that were unknown. As they tested the unknown material to determine its chemical makeup, they realized they had not just discovered a new element.

They had discovered *two* new elements.

The Curies prepared to write a scientific paper about the first element, and Pierre asked Marie what she wanted to name it. Her thoughts turned once again to Poland, a country that no longer officially existed.

Marie said, "Could we call it 'polonium'?"

The Curies officially announced the discovery of polonium in July 1898 in the *Proceedings of the Academy*, a scientific publication of the French Academy of Sciences. Part of it read, "We propose to call it *polonium*, from the name of the original country of one of us."

Marie immediately sent the manuscript that was published in the French journal to her cousin Joseph Boguski, who ran the laboratory behind the title of "museum" in Warsaw. He had made it possible for Marie to work in a laboratory for the first time only seven years before. Joseph saw to it that Marie and Pierre's paper was published in Poland, even though it had to be printed in a Warsaw photographic review instead of a scientific journal where it belonged.

In July 1898, the same month polonium was announced to the world, Marie recorded in her notebook at home that ten-month-old Irène could say "Gogli, gogli, go" and that she could "roll, pick herself up, and sit down." During the months that followed, not only was Marie making notes at work about the second unknown element, she was still making notes at home in her cookbooks. Beside the recipe for gooseberry jelly, she noted that eight pounds of fruit had produced "fourteen pots of very good jelly."

The second new element was announced publicly on December 26, 1898, when the French Academy of Sciences published a paper titled "On a New, Strongly Radioactive Substance Contained in Pitchblende." Three people were given credit for the article: Pierre Curie, Marie Curie, and Gustave Bémont, head of chemical operations at the School of Physics and Chemistry. The paper said that the radioactive substances they worked on contained "a new element to which we propose to give the name of RADIUM." The Curies chose the name *radium* because the Latin word for "ray" is *radius*.

Marie switched back and forth between being a scientist and being a mother. Ten days after radium's discovery was announced, she noted that Irène had fifteen teeth.

The Curies could demonstrate the existence of polonium and radium in the laboratory, yet neither element had yet been seen. To prove their dis-

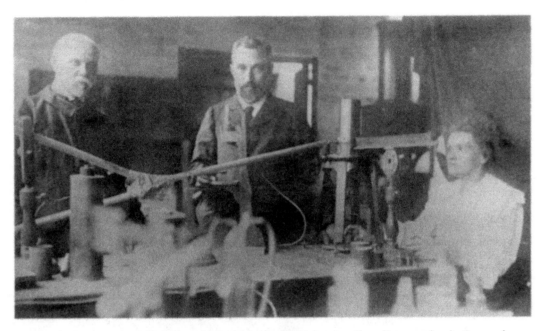

Pierre and Marie in their shed-turned-laboratory in 1898, the year they discovered polonium and radium. On the left is Petit, Pierre's laboratory assistant, who helped them whenever he could. The instrument between the Curies is the piezoelectric quartz electrometer that had been invented by Pierre and his brother, Jacques.

covery to their fellow chemists, the Curies needed to isolate enough of each from pitchblende to pinpoint its atomic weight (the weight of one atom of an element). It would be difficult to do, since radium and polonium were found only in tiny amounts mixed in with other materials.

Pierre and Marie realized they would need a ton or more of pitchblende and much more space to process it. Marie described their dilemma: "We had no money, no suitable laboratory, no personal help for our great and difficult undertaking. It was like creating something out of nothing."

Pierre's boss helped them again by allowing them to use the only vacant place on school property—another empty shed. In the past it had been used by medical students to dissect cadavers; then it wasn't even considered good enough for storage. However, it was conveniently located right across the courtyard from the glassed-in room that Pierre and Marie had turned into their laboratory.

The Curies were happy to accept the offer. Marie described it as a wooden shed with "a glass roof which did not keep the rain out . . . The only objects it contained were some worn pine tables, a cast-iron stove, which worked badly, and the blackboard which Pierre Curie loved to use."

So they needed pitchblende, and it had to be cheap. Their only income was from Pierre's teaching job, which he continued in addition to his work with Marie. The research on radium and polonium was done with their own money and time.

The Academy of Sciences in Vienna, Austria, helped them locate a cheap source for pitchblende. The Austrian government operated a uranium mine in St. Joachimsthal, a place known today as Jáchymov and located in what is now the Czech Republic. At the time, uranium was used to make beautifully colored glassware. After the uranium was removed from the pitchblende, the material left behind was considered useless and tossed on the ground. But the radium and polonium were still there. The Austrian government donated the pitchblende, so that Pierre and Marie only had to dip into their small savings account to pay for its transport to Paris.

When the wagonload of pitchblende arrived, Marie raced out to see it without stopping to take off her laboratory apron. She couldn't wait to get her hands on it as the sacks were unloaded. She opened one sack and dug her hands into the heavy, dark brown powder still littered with pine needles from the forest floor.

This worthless-looking material contained radium and polonium. Now all Marie and Pierre had to do was separate these two elements from everything else. But how? Isolating an element that existed in such tiny amounts would be a difficult task. There were no instructions, no books, and no experts who could help.

Each member of the Curie team had a different strength. Marie, who always counted in Polish, was a mathematics expert. Her job was to extract and purify the radium. Pierre had many years of experience in laboratory research. His job was to study the physical properties of radium as Marie produced it.

Where should she start?

First she boiled the pitchblende with an acid used for cleaning and bleaching. Day after day Marie worked in the courtyard, stirring a bubbling pot with a rod that was almost as tall as she was. The back-breaking work left her tired. She said she "had to work with as much as twenty kilogrammes [about forty-four pounds] of material at a time, so that the hangar was filled with great vessels full of precipitates [substances separated from a solution] and of liquids. It was exhausting work to move the containers about, to transfer the liquids, and to stir for hours at a time, with an iron bar, the boiling material in the cast-iron basin." The process finally resulted in a residue of radium mixed in with various metals. At this point, Marie decided that since radium was more radioactive than polonium, it would be the element on which she would focus.

Next she boiled the residue with a different solution and repeatedly washed it with water to get rid of some of the metals. She treated the remaining residue with another boiling solution, washed it with water, and treated it with corrosive agents. Because radium seemed chemically similar to the metallic element barium, additional processes enabled her to separate out radium sulfate and barium sulfate. (A sulfate results when sulfur and oxygen combine with another material to make a usually acidic substance.)

After that, Marie boiled the radium sulfate and barium sulfate residue, turning it into radium salt. She treated the radium salt extensively, using one process after another.

Even for a scientist such as Marie Curie, it was an enormously complicated process.

The next step required even more tedious work.

Throughout 1899 Marie used fractional crystallization, a method of separating components using their different chemical properties, to separate other substances from the radium salt. Working with one small batch at a time, she added distilled water and boiled it, then allowed it to cool and crystallize. She collected the resulting radioactive crystals and took them through the purification process again and again. It took thousands of steps of fractional crystallization to remove other substances from each batch, further purifying the radium each time. And the more pure the radium salt became, the more radioactive it became.

When she began her work, Marie estimated that radium made up one percent of pitchblende. In reality, radium made up only one millionth of one percent of the ore. One mere gram of radium could be gotten out of seven tons of pitchblende. That's like getting the weight of three raisins out of an adult elephant.

Even though the work was extremely demanding, the Curies both loved it. Marie had never been happier:

We were very happy in spite of the difficult conditions under which we worked. We passed our days at the laboratory, often eating a simple student's lunch there. A great tranquillity reigned in our poor, shabby hangar; occasionally, while observing an operation, we would walk up and down talking of our work, present and future. When we were cold, a cup of hot tea, drunk

beside the stove, cheered us. We lived in a preoccupation as complete as that
of a dream.

The poor conditions of the laboratory became a problem for Marie at this stage of her work. She needed her equipment to be at a consistent temperature to ensure accurate measurements. She also needed a clean laboratory so dust wouldn't contaminate her radium samples.

Understanding the difficulty of the job ahead of them, Pierre suggested they postpone their goal of further isolating and purifying radium salt until they had a better laboratory in which to work.

He underestimated Marie's determination and persistence. She would not consider leaving her work simply because it would be hard. Marie had set out to isolate radium, and she would do it. Nothing was going to stop her.

By 1900, the Curie family (Pierre, Marie, Irène, and Dr. Curie, Pierre's father) had moved out of their apartment and into a house. Around that time the University of Geneva in Switzerland offered Pierre an important job with a higher salary. The university promised to build a laboratory for him and give Marie an official position in it. Marie and Pierre visited and liked Geneva. They were tempted by the chance to have a decent laboratory. But Pierre knew a move would interrupt their work with radium for a while, and he knew Marie especially didn't want that to happen. He refused the job even though their family could have used the extra income, since their work with radium was costing them money rather than bringing any in.

Knowing the Curies' situation, Henri Poincaré, a well-known mathematician and physicist, helped Pierre get a job at the Sorbonne teaching a class of medical students. Pierre took this on in addition to his regular professorship at the School of Physics and Chemistry.

And Marie got a job teaching physics to young women in the nearby town of Sèvres, at the Normale Supérieure School. Although it took time away from her laboratory work, she liked teaching science to those who were preparing to become teachers themselves.

The work on radium continued at a slow but steady pace. Pierre looked forward to the day when Marie would have isolated enough radium salt so that they could see it with their own eyes. He hoped it would be a beautiful color.

After tucking Irène into bed one evening, Marie picked up the latest dress she was hand-sewing for her daughter. But she just couldn't concentrate on her stitches. She suggested to Pierre that they return to the laboratory.

They walked through the streets of Paris and let themselves into the darkened lab. Since they were familiar with every inch of the place, they didn't bother to light the lamps. Immediately they made their way toward the rough wooden shelves that held the product of years of work. Glass tubes contained the few particles of radium salt Marie had been able to produce.

Then they saw it. It was even more beautiful than Pierre had hoped it would be.

Radium glowed in the dark.

Together Pierre and Marie sat in the darkness and gazed at the wonderful sight. Marie thought the glow looked like "faint, fairy lights."

Marie and Pierre would never forget this magical moment.

Many nights after the first one, they would return to the lab to admire their "precious products." Marie said, "From all sides we could see their slightly luminous silhouettes, and these gleamings, which seemed suspended in the darkness, stirred us with ever new emotion and enchantment."

Marie succeeded at last. It took her four years to extract one decigram (one tenth of a gram) of radium in the form of a salt (not pure radium metal) from pitchblende. It was a tiny amount, but it was pure enough to determine its atomic weight, a necessary step in establishing radium as a new element. She weighed her minute sample on an extremely accurate scale previously created by Pierre. In her laboratory

In the dark, the glow of radium salt in this bowl illuminates the surrounding area with enough light to read by. With the lights on, radium salt looked almost like table salt.

notebook, she noted on March 28, 1902, "Ra=225.93. The weight of an atom of radium." (She was remarkably close: the true weight is 226.0254.)

At the time, the world of science believed that atoms of elements were unchangeable. As the Curies continued their work and published papers on what they'd discovered about radium and radioactivity, their findings inspired many other scientists to study radioactivity. Ernest Rutherford (who would be awarded the 1908 Nobel Prize in Chemistry) and Frederick Soddy (who would be awarded the 1921 Nobel Prize in Chemistry) proved that the atoms of radioactive elements were constantly changing, even transforming from one element into a completely different one. Their research demonstrated that as atoms of radioactive elements change from one element into another in what is known as the decay process, they release energy (radioactivity). Half-life is the amount of time it takes for one half of the atoms of a radioactive material to decay (transform) into the atoms of a different element.

The half-life of each radioactive element is different: some have a half-life of a fraction of a second; some, billions of years. The half-life of radium is 1,620 years. For example, if you had eight grams of radium, in 1,620 years you would have four grams of radium; 1,620 years later you would have two grams of radium; and 1,620 years after that, one gram. On and on the decay process would go.

The Curies sent samples of radium to important scientists of the day, including Henri Becquerel and Great Britain's William Thomson, Lord Kelvin. Because of their generosity in allowing others to study radium, knowledge about radioactivity was able to expand quickly.

As scientists all over the world began to study radium, some of what they learned would enable it to become useful to society. Friedrich Dorn, a German chemist, discovered that radium emitted a radioactive gas that he called radium emanation, later known as another new element: radon. Radon has a half-life of 3.82 days.

In 1900, two German scientists, Otto Walkhoff and Friedrich Giesel, reported that exposure to radium caused changes in the human body. To test their findings, Pierre Curie attached a vial of radium salt to his lower arm for ten hours to see what would happen. He reported the results to the French Academy of Sciences in June 1901. An area of skin about two and one-half inches square turned red as if it were burned. On day twenty it scabbed over; on day forty-two the skin began to heal around the edges; and by day fifty-two it was a deep wound about a half-inch across whose gray appearance indicated the tissue was dead. Pierre also reported that his fingertips, as well as Marie's, had "become hard and sometimes very painful" from handling radium.

Since radium had caused tissue death, Pierre wondered if it could be used to treat cancer. X-ray therapy was already being used with great success, and maybe radium could help even more. After further research,

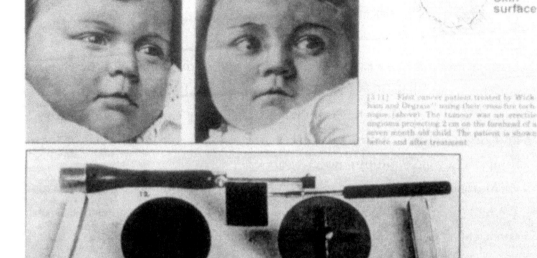

Skin surface

[5.11] First cancer patient treated by Wickham and Degrais using their cross-fire technique (above). The tumour was an erectile angioma projecting 2 cm on the forehead of a seven month old child. The patient is shown before and after treatment.

Before and after radium therapy was used to get rid of this angioma, a kind of tumor, for cosmetic reasons. In addition to cancer treatment, radium therapy was used on various conditions that were not life-threatening. Below are some instruments used in radium therapy.

Pierre and some medical doctors agreed to try it out. Samples supplied by the Curies were used in the first cancer treatment using radium. The treatment became known as curietherapy.

Because radium could be placed on the outside of the body near the cancer, it was especially helpful for skin cancer. But most cancers are located deep within the patient's body. Alexander Graham Bell, the inventor of the telephone, was one of the first to propose radium's use internally: "There is no reason why a tiny fragment of radium sealed up in a fine glass tube should not be inserted into the very heart of the cancer." This method proved successful in many cases.

When it was learned that radium could be used to treat cancer, the entire world was suddenly interested in it.

Marie and Pierre could have gotten patents on their radium and the process they used to extract it. If they had, anyone who used their radium or their method of extraction would have had to pay money to the Curies.

They could have been rich. They could have built themselves a fancy laboratory. They could have quit their jobs. They could have gone home and never worked another day in their lives. They didn't do any of these things. They gave radium away.

Marie said they "refused to draw any material profit from our discovery. We took no copyright, and published without reserve all the results of our research, as well as the exact processes of the preparation of radium. In addition, we gave to those interested whatever information they asked of us." The Curies were more concerned about what they could do for humankind than about what humankind could do for them.

Marie had been delighted to share with her father that she'd been successful at isolating enough radium to determine its atomic weight. Yet only a few weeks later her father died.

She was brokenhearted. She couldn't forget that she'd once promised him she would return to Poland and live with him after her education was complete. Instead, she'd married Pierre and stayed in France to do her

Radium therapy needles contained either radium or radon (the gas emitted from radium) and were placed directly into a cancer deep inside a patient's body. With this method, the amount of radiation to surrounding healthy tissues was less than when the radioactive source was placed on the skin. The tube on the left was used to carry radioactive needles.

research. Her father had understood, but Marie couldn't forgive herself.

In addition to her grief, the strain of the past four years was beginning to show. Since her work began, Marie had lost fifteen pounds from her already thin frame. Ignoring her exhaustion, she pushed herself to get everything done. She'd dash back and forth between her laboratory, her teaching job in Sèvres, and her young daughter, Irène. Added to that, Marie had begun work on her research thesis to earn her doctorate. She didn't even rest on weekends. Since their home had a cozy garden, it became a gathering place for friends. While everyone chatted, Marie, who made all of Irène's dresses, caught up on her hand-sewing.

By April 1903, Georges Sagnac, a friend and physicist, was worried about Marie. He wrote Pierre, saying, "I have been struck, when I have seen Mme Curie at the Society of Physics, by the alteration in her appearance. I know very well that she is overworked because of her thesis . . . you hardly eat at all, either of you. More than once I have seen Mme Curie nibble two slices of sausage and swallow a cup of tea with it . . . What would become of you if Mme Curie lost her health?"

Marie and Pierre assured Sagnac they would catch up on their rest during the summer vacation. But they didn't tell their friend how they spent their time. The Curies spent each vacation riding their bicycles through the French countryside. If they stayed in one place more than a couple of days, Pierre suggested they return to Paris, saying, "We have been doing nothing for a long time now."

Marie was unconcerned about her own health, but she worried about Pierre's. He'd been having attacks of inexplicable pain, mostly in his legs. Doctors thought it might be rheumatism, although they weren't entirely sure. Many a night he tossed and turned in agony in his bed. While Pierre moaned in misery, Marie fretted over him, unable to help.

On one of those pain-filled nights, the fear that had been growing in Marie finally came out in words. She said, "Pierre . . . if one of us disappeared . . . We can't exist without each other, can we?"

Pierre's answer was clear: "You are wrong. Whatever happens, even if one has to go on like a body without a soul, one must work just the same."

Neither Pierre nor Marie imagined that radium, their precious discovery, might be making him sick. When she wrote of Pierre's illness twenty years later, Marie said, "The physical fatigue due to the numerous courses he was obliged to give was so great that he suffered from attacks of acute pain, which in his overtaxed condition became more and more frequent."

In June 1903, Pierre was invited to London to give a lecture on radium at the Royal Institution. Since Marie was a woman, she could not speak to the all-male group. No woman before Marie had ever been permitted even to attend a lecture there. The Royal Institution made an exception for Marie since she was the co-discoverer of radium. She was *allowed* to sit in the audience beside Great Britain's famous scientist Lord Kelvin.

Women of Marie's day had few rights. They were not allowed to vote, and just to open a bank account they needed their husband's approval. Marie was the only woman at her level of education and experience in a field of science made up of men. She was often way ahead of her male counterparts, yet many of them would never accept her as a serious scientist because of her gender. Although Marie was opening doors of opportunity for women in science who would come after her, she was not a feminist or crusader for women's rights. All she cared about was her work, and she thought of herself as a scientist, not as a woman scientist.

On the evening of the lecture at the Royal Institution, Pierre was visibly ill. His legs were trembling as he dressed in the threadbare black suit he wore when he taught class. His fingers were so raw and cracked from radium burns that he couldn't button his vest; Marie had to do it.

Pierre discussed the properties of radium and showed the audience the sore on his arm caused by radium two years before. He also demonstrated some scientific experiments using radium. During his presentation, Pierre accidentally spilled a bit of their precious element. Fifty years later the room was discovered to be still radioactive and had to be decontaminated.

Back in France later that month, Marie—who was expecting another baby—prepared to defend her doctoral thesis. It had been almost twelve years since she'd begun her university education and five years since she'd begun her work on radium. Three of her own physics professors from the Sorbonne questioned the co-discoverer of radium about her work. She explained what she had done alone and what Pierre had done.

Marie earned her doctorate on June 25, 1903. She was the first woman in France to do so.

Manya Sklodowska, the shy little girl who had dissolved into tears when called on in class, had become Dr. Marie Sklodowska Curie.

But only a few weeks afterward, Marie and Pierre's second daughter died shortly after birth. Grief overwhelmed Marie again. Since Bronya and her family had previously moved back to Poland to run a sanatorium for tuberculosis patients, Marie shared the sad news with her sister by letter. On August 25, 1903, Marie wrote, "I had grown so accustomed to the idea of the child that I am absolutely desperate and cannot be consoled. Write to me, I beg of you, if you think I should blame this on general fatigue—for I must admit that I have not spared my strength."

While Marie agonized over the loss of her baby, radium became famous.

FAME

News of the unusual characteristics of radium spread outside scientific circles and into public awareness. In early 1903, articles had begun to appear in newspapers about the success of using radium to treat cancer and possible ways it might be used in the future.

By the fall of that year there was enough interest in radium that when a small amount was donated to the American Museum of Natural History in New York City and put on display, large crowds gathered to see it. As people shuffled past to get a look at radium enclosed in tiny glass capsules, most were disappointed. The yellowish powder didn't look special at all.

But to scientists, radium was more than special. It was considered a miracle for many reasons: it constantly emanated radon gas; it could treat diseases; its temperature was always warmer than that of the surrounding air; and it never lost its power.

The discovery of radium was honored on December 10, 1903, when Marie, Pierre, and Henri Becquerel were awarded the Nobel Prize in Physics.

Marie Curie was the first woman to win a Nobel Prize and also the first Polish person to win one.

Nobel winners were expected to travel to Stockholm, Sweden, to receive the prestigious prize and give a lecture. But Marie and Pierre were both too sick to go. It's likely the radium they were being honored for was partly the cause of many of their health problems. Marie was weak with exhaustion and grief. Pierre battled unexplained pain and trembling in his legs. They assured the Nobel Prize committee they would travel there at a later date to give the lecture.

It was not known publicly until the 1980s, when the Nobel archives were opened, that Marie had not even been nominated to win the prize that year. Only Pierre Curie and Henri Becquerel were nominated for their work on radioactivity. One of the Swedish physicists on the committee wrote Pierre that he alone was considered for the prize, without Marie. Pierre had never cared for prizes or honors for himself, but he wanted Marie to have the recognition she deserved. Pierre wrote back, "If it is true that one is seriously thinking about me [for the prize], I very much wish to be considered together with Madame Curie with respect to our research on radioactive bodies."

Fortunately, Marie's name had been submitted for consideration the year before. Because of this, the Royal Swedish Academy of Sciences allowed Marie to be named along with her husband for the Nobel Prize they shared with Becquerel.

The award carried with it a diploma, gold medals, and a cash prize, and it brought its winners worldwide fame. The $40,000 prize money was halved between the Curies and Becquerel.

The Curies, who had always struggled with lack of money, used some of their $20,000 to hire a lab assistant. They also generously gave money to friends and family who were in need. Neither Marie nor Pierre bought even the smallest gift for themselves, but they did repaper a room in their home and install a modern bathroom.

With extra money for the first time in her life, Marie remembered Madame Kozlowska, one of her childhood teachers. Madame Kozlowska, who was French, had married a Polish man and had lived in Poland ever since. Marie recalled how her teacher longed to see her beloved France again but could not afford to travel there. Marie understood how her teacher felt: Madame Kozlowska yearned for France, just as Marie had for Poland.

Marie provided Madame Kozlowska with the trip of her dreams. She paid her travel expenses to and from France and invited her to stay in the Curie home during her visit.

Marie never forgot a kindness that had been done for her, or a wrong that had been done to her.

After they won the Nobel Prize, news reports about and photographs of the Curies spread all over the world. Their story captured the interest of people everywhere: a poor Polish woman beat all odds to get an education in Paris; she fell in love with a renowned scientist and worked with him for four years in a pitiful shed where they discovered a new element, which could be used to treat cancer; and then they won a Nobel Prize.

Marie and Pierre were suddenly famous. They hated it.

The days of working together in solitude had come to an end. Peace and quiet for them became as rare as their radium. Uninvited visitors began dropping by their laboratory. They were overwhelmed by letters of congratulation, honors for their work, questions from fellow scientists, requests for interviews, invitations to lecture, requests for autographs and photographs, and even requests for loans. There were letters containing poems about radium, and one asking permission to name a racehorse after Marie. The media frenzy surrounding them made it impossible for Marie and Pierre to get any work done.

In a letter to her brother in February 1904, Marie complained that their life had been "altogether spoiled by honors and fame."

The Curies' lives would never be the same again. From this point on, if anyone recognized Marie in public and asked, "Aren't you Madame Curie?" she would answer, "No, you are mistaken." In an attempt to

Marie and Pierre Curie working in their laboratory in 1904, a few months after being awarded their Nobel Prize. They didn't like the fame that followed.

maintain their privacy, the Curies registered under a false name whenever they went on vacation. But even that didn't always keep reporters away.

One American journalist tracked them down while they were vacationing at a cottage in Le Pouldu, in southern Brittany. He happened to find Marie on the doorstep as she was shaking sand out of her beach shoes. He took out his notebook and began asking her questions about her work. She answered his questions about radium. But when he inquired about her personal life, she ended the interview by saying, "In science we must be interested in things, not in persons."

Although people all over the world valued the Curies' work, recognition from their peers in France was slow in coming. After the Nobel Prize, Pierre continued his full-time teaching job at the School of Physics and Chemistry in addition to his part-time teaching job at the Sorbonne. Almost a year passed before the Sorbonne offered to create a position of professor of physics for Pierre. He accepted and was allowed to hire three workers: an assistant, a lab boy, and a laboratory chief. Marie was named his laboratory chief. For the first time in her career, Marie would be regularly paid for her scientific research.

The Sorbonne also promised to build Pierre a laboratory.

The leaky shed-turned-laboratory where Pierre and Marie had discovered radium belonged to the School of Physics and Chemistry. When Pierre left there to teach full-time at the Sorbonne, they had to leave their beloved shed behind. The shed held a special place in Marie's heart in spite of its poor conditions. She said, "We had become particularly attached to our hangar, which continued to stand, though in a state of increasing decay, for several years, and we went to visit it from time to time."

Not only were the Curies famous now; so was radium. In fact, radium seemed to take on a life of its own. Newspaper articles suggested uses for radium that were outright ridiculous: to prevent rabies in dogs, to determine the sex of an unborn baby, to explode bombs from long distance, to cure insanity, and to induce chickens to lay hard-boiled eggs.

A *New York Times* article on January 14, 1904, reported that Dr. William J. Morton, a prominent New York City doctor, had demonstrated a radium concoction he called "liquid sunshine." Dr. Morton was quoted as saying that with his mixture it would be possible "to bathe a patient's entire interior in violet or ultra violet light as the result of this discovery, and this light we have decided to call 'sunshine.'"

On May 8, 1904, a *Times* article said:

> *There seems to be hardly any limit to the marvels of radium. A French person of science . . . affirms that its heat rays are capable of melting down stones and massive iron and steel structures and that its qualities must interdict all war. In the fierceness of its rays forts must dissolve, great warships dissipate, and soldiers curl up and die like leaves in a forest fire.*

After the Curies discovered radium, naturally occurring hot springs around the world were tested and found to be radioactive. For centuries people had traveled to the springs believing the water could cure their ailments, but no one had known why.

Many reasoned that if radioactive water was good for your health, then maybe everyone should be drinking it. Since most people didn't live near a natural radioactive spring, why not create a device to make radium water in your own home, no matter where you lived?

A new business was born.

One of many companies that produced crocks to make radium water at home was the Radium Ore Company. It claimed its radioactive water was

Ridiculous articles like these led people to think radium was the answer to almost any problem.
Fascination with radium was so widespread that Columbia University provided a booth at the
1904 St. Louis World's Fair with a section showing various uses for radium.

"equal to the average of the most famous health springs, among which are included Hot Springs, Ark." This company claimed radium water improved health because it had a "peculiar force of ejecting poisons from the organs of the body . . . Any water that has lost its original radio-activity by being bottled or flowing through reservoirs and pipes to a faucet is, of course, almost entirely minus this health element of radio-activity." A water jar from the company promised to restore "the lost element of original freshness—radio-activity, to water" and to allow sick people to "throw off ailments of long standing and to be restored to real health."

Another way to make radium water at home

Centuries before radium was discovered, various tribes of American Indians considered the water in what is now Hot Springs, Arkansas, neutral territory. All could go there to bathe in and drink the healing water in peace. This 1905 postcard shows a crowd gathered to drink the slightly radioactive water. It is described as the "Daily Drinking Scene at John W. Noble Fountain." People today still flock to Hot Springs to visit the bathhouses and fill containers with drinking water.

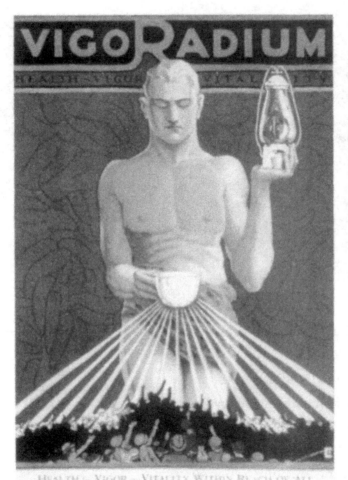

The inside lining of the Revigator jar contained traces of radium. Water sitting in the crock became radioactive by absorbing radon gas given off by the radium. In 1926, this crock would have sold for $29.50. More than a half million Revigator crocks were sold. Directions were printed on the side of the jar: "1. Fill jar every night. 2. Use hydrant or any good water. 3. Drink freely when thirsty and upon arising and retiring. Average six or more glasses daily."

This advertisement for VigoRadium shows masses of people reaching out for the "health," "vigor," and "vitality" it offered. The product made radium water one cup at a time. Water placed in the glass globe was irradiated by the radium source sealed inside it. Radioactive water was then served from the spigot into a cup. VigoRadium's brochure said, "Everyone who's able should have it on the table."

was to place a radium-containing device in any container of water. The Thomas Radioactive Cone was one of these products. It was about five inches high and made from a mixture of concrete and radioactive ore. An advertisement for the Thomas Cone said, "Children who drink this water will probably never have ulcers, tumors, cancers, or goiter."

No matter what style or shape, all radium water devices worked the same way: they exposed water to radon, which caused it to become slightly radioactive for a few days.

TROUBLE

While people around the world were trying to figure out how to make money from radium products, the two who discovered it were not. Marie and Pierre did not approve of or participate in using radium in any way other than for science.

But letters poured in from people with ideas about how to use radium who wanted their help. The Curies ignored these letters—except for one.

A letter arrived from Loie Fuller, an American dancer in Paris who was well known for her performances using colored electric lighting. When Fuller heard that radium glowed in the dark, she was planning her next dance and costume. She wrote the Curies to ask them if she could use radium on the butterfly wings of her costume. They were so amused by her letter, they took time to write to Fuller and explain that it would be impossible to use the element in this way.

To thank the Curies for answering her letter, Fuller offered to perform one of her famous dances in their home. They agreed. Fuller and her lighting team worked all day to prepare the Curies' dining room for her performance. That evening the Curies and a few friends had a private show.

An unlikely friendship developed between the dancer and the two Nobel laureates, who visited back and forth at one another's homes. Through Fuller, the Curies met and became friends with people they would not have met otherwise, such as Auguste Rodin, the renowned French sculptor.

Even as the Curies were adjusting to being in the public eye, their private lives were changing again. On December 6, 1904, Marie gave birth to another daughter, Eve Denise. As when Irène was born, neither Marie nor Pierre considered the possibility that Marie would stop working; Pierre's father offered to care for the children while Marie did her research.

When women asked how she was able to balance a family and a scientific career, Marie answered, "It has not been easy; it required a great deal of decision and of self-sacrifice."

Meanwhile, Marie and Pierre's work with radium continued to affect their health. In a letter to his friend the scientist Georges Gouy, at the end of January 1905, Pierre wrote, "To tell the truth, I can only keep up by avoiding all physical fatigue. And my wife is in the same condition; we can no longer dream of the great work days of times gone by."

But by the summer of 1905, Pierre felt strong enough to travel to Stockholm to give the long-awaited Nobel Prize lecture. In June, a year and a half after winning the award, Pierre delivered his lecture on radium while Marie sat in the audience. As usual, Pierre was careful to explain which part of the work on radium had been done by Marie alone and which they had accomplished together.

It must have been good for them to get away from their work for a while. Not long after their trip, Pierre wrote to a friend on July 24, 1905, "Our children and my father are very well, and my wife and I are much better, although we get tired easily."

Still, by the fall of 1905, Marie and Pierre found themselves frustrated. The laboratory that the Sorbonne had promised to build more than a year before wasn't forthcoming. They had given Pierre an allowance to put toward a lab, but it wasn't enough to build the kind they needed. The Curies had to settle for a two-room laboratory on Rue Cuvier, not far from their beloved leaky shed.

Pierre's health seemed to decline all through the year. In another letter to Georges Gouy dated November 7, 1905, he wrote:

I am neither very well, nor very ill; but I am easily fatigued, and I have left but very little capacity for work. My wife, on the contrary, leads a very active life, between her children, the School at Sèvres, and the laboratory. She does not lose a minute, and occupies herself more regularly than I can with the direction of the laboratory in which she passes the greater part of the day.

In April 1906, Pierre was "quite ill and tired" when he, Marie, Irène, and Eve spent the Easter holiday in the French countryside. For two days,

Marie and Pierre enjoyed the spring flowers, watched their children play, and took walks with them in the woods.

As usual, Pierre was anxious to return to work, so he planned to leave a day earlier than Marie and the children. When he caught the late train back to Paris, he carried with him a bouquet of fresh buttercups he'd picked in the country.

On April 19, the day after Marie returned from the country, a cold spring rain drenched the narrow streets of Paris. Both Marie and Pierre had a busy day ahead.

Pierre hurried from one appointment to the next. In a downpour at about two-thirty that afternoon, Pierre was walking down Rue Dauphine toward the Seine River, under his umbrella. The street was bustling with horse-drawn traffic of all kinds. The narrow sidewalks full of people slowed Pierre's progress as he made his way through the rain. To get away from the crowds, he stepped into the slippery street to follow an enclosed carriage.

Although the carriage obscured his view of oncoming traffic, Pierre suddenly stepped to the left from behind it to cross the street. He didn't see the horse-drawn wagon coming toward him until it was too late. He tried to hold on to the horses but fell instead.

The rear wheel of the wagon ran over his skull and crushed it. He died instantly.

Marie didn't know what had happened as she hurried home that evening; she didn't know her life was about to change forever. Friends who had gathered at the house told Marie about Pierre.

She sat motionless.

Silence.

After a few minutes, she mumbled, "Pierre is dead? Dead? Absolutely dead?"

The dry-eyed new widow numbly requested that Pierre's body be brought back to their home.

Marie noticed that in the study the buttercups Pierre had brought back from the country were still fresh.

She stumbled out to the garden, wet with rain, and sat down. With her elbows on her knees and her head held in her hands, she waited for Pierre's body.

Marie sent eight-year-old Irène to stay with a neighbor, telling her that her father had hurt his head and needed rest. Eve was allowed to stay at home, since at sixteen months she was too young to understand what was happening.

Marie arranged for Pierre to be buried beside his mother in Sceaux. She insisted Pierre's service be simple, without speeches and public intrusion, as he would have wanted.

But there would be no privacy even for this occasion. On the day of Pierre's funeral, journalists hid in the cemetery to watch Marie's every move. An article in *Le Journal* on April 22, 1906, reported:

Mme Curie, on her father-in-law's arm, followed her husband's coffin to the tomb hollowed out at the foot of the wall of the enclosure in the shadow of the chestnut trees. There she remained motionless for a moment, always with the same fixed, hard gaze; but when a sheaf of flowers was brought near the tomb, she seized it with a sudden movement and began to detach the flowers one by one to scatter them on the coffin. She did this slowly, composedly, and seemed to have totally forgotten the audience, which, profoundly struck, made no noise, no murmur . . . Then, allowing the bouquet she held to fall to the earth, she left the tomb without saying a word and rejoined her father-in-law.

The day after Pierre's funeral, Marie told Irène that her father was dead.

Although Marie's grief ran deep, she would not allow herself to weep in public. She poured her despair into the privacy of her diary.

On the Sunday morning after your death, Pierre, I went to the laboratory with Jacques for the first time. I tried to make a measurement, for a graph on which we had each made several points. But I felt the impossibility of going on.

In the street I walk as if hypnotized, without attending to anything. I shall not kill myself. I have not even the desire for suicide. But among all these vehicles is there not one to make me share the fate of my beloved?

Marie could not bear to talk about Pierre, not even to mention his name. In the years following his death, she would never talk to her daughters about their father.

Around this time, Marie began rubbing together her fingertips and thumbs (which had become hard from working with vials of radium) in a nervous habit. Unconsciously, she would rub and rub and rub. The habit stayed with her for the rest of her life.

But she remembered Pierre's words: "Whatever happens, even if one has to go on like a body without a soul, one must work just the same."

The French government offered her a pension, but she refused to take the money. At thirty-nine years old, Marie said, "I don't want a pension. I am young enough to earn my living and that of my children."

Pierre's death left a hole at the Sorbonne, too. Who could replace him in his class and laboratory?

Only one person was qualified to continue Pierre's work: Marie Curie. The Sorbonne asked Marie to take over Pierre's job when school started in the fall, and she accepted.

But Marie was unprepared for the next blow.

Pierre had been dead for only a few months when Marie sent her children on a summer vacation without her. Irène went with their Aunt Hela, who had come to France to help them, and Eve traveled with their grandfather. Marie stayed home to study Pierre's notes to prepare herself to take over his classes at the Sorbonne.

Lord Kelvin, a friend and past supporter of Pierre's, wrote an article that summer that appeared in the London *Times*. In it, he stated that he did not believe radium was an element, only a compound of other elements.

The work that had consumed Marie for years was now being publicly challenged by one of the oldest and most respected scientists of the day. What should she do?

Marie was exhausted with grief. Her children needed her, her laboratory needed her, her students needed her, Pierre's students needed her, her radium needed her. And she needed Pierre.

Some people believed that Marie had been only Pierre's assistant, instead of his equal partner. Now she had to prove herself a scientist in her own right. She had to defend the work on radium that she and Pierre had accomplished.

She refused to argue publicly against Lord Kelvin and his claim. There was only one thing to do—continue her work on radium without Pierre.

First, she needed to make a few changes. She quit her job as teacher at the girls' school in Sèvres and moved her family, including Pierre's father, back to Sceaux. Marie could not bear to live without Pierre in the house in Paris where they had been so happy together. Living on the outskirts of Paris meant Marie had a half-hour train ride to and from the lab each day. But it was worth it to be near Pierre's grave.

As fall approached, she had to get through the first day of teaching his class.

Her initial class, on November 5, 1906, was historic. No woman had ever taught at the Sorbonne before. Reporters, friends, strangers, and students squeezed into the lecture hall to see what the famous widow would do.

Marie visited Pierre's grave before class. Despite her personal grief, she entered the classroom promptly at one-thirty. The crowd honored her with thunderous applause. She steadied herself by holding on to the equipment table. When the room was quiet, she began, "When one considers the progress that has been made in physics in the past ten years . . ." Marie had begun her first lecture at the exact place where Pierre had stopped his last.

Françoise Giroud's book *Marie Curie: A Life* contains a quote from a man who described Marie that day. She had "a strange face, ageless. Her light and deep eyes seemed tired from having read too much or cried too much."

When she finished, the crowd roared their appreciation.

But Marie's focus was on the work on radium that was ahead of her and the decisions she must make regarding her children. Though Eve was still a baby, Irène was old enough to begin her education. Marie did not like that schoolchildren in France were expected to sit in a classroom all day long with little physical activity. So she organized parents who were fellow scientists to band together to educate their own children. An incredible group of parents agreed to teach the ten children. These parents included Jean Perrin (who would win a Nobel Prize in Physics in 1926 for his work on the structure of matter) and Paul Langevin (a previous student of Pierre's and friend to both Curies, whose later work on ultrasonic vibrations to detect submarines during World War I led to the development of sonar in World War II). The hope was that the children would learn only one lesson each day, but each lesson would be taught by a master in that field. For two years, the group practiced in this way until the workload for the adults became too heavy and the time came for the children to go to an official school.

Marie wanted her daughters to have a good education in math, science, and sports, but there were areas that she completely ignored. She made a decision not to give them any type of religious instruction, with the idea that when they were adults they could be free to decide for themselves. Marie also failed to teach her children good manners. Most people considered Irène to be rude. In the biography of her mother titled *Madame Curie*, Eve wrote: "When Irène met strangers, she was panic-stricken, she became completely mute, and obstinately refused to 'say how do you do to the lady.' She would never completely get over this habit of hers."

Marie did not show physical affection to her daughters, probably because her own mother, owing to her illness, had not been able to hug and kiss Marie. Yet she loved them dearly. Marie taught her daughters that they must not be afraid of the dark, or storms, or the bad things that happen in life. They were not allowed to raise their voices either when happy or sad. Eve remembered that her mother rarely disciplined them, but when she did, it was not in the traditional way. Once, to punish Irène, Marie decided not to speak to her for two days. Another time, when Marie was helping

Irène with her studies and Irène gave the wrong answer, Marie threw her notebook out the window.

Each of her daughters was different in personality. Irène had a mind for science and was destined to become famous in her own right, whereas Eve was interested in music and writing.

While Marie was busy with her children and her work, radium factories were being built all over the world based on information the Curies had freely shared. On May 3, 1908, *The New York Times* reported on a visit to a factory in France:

Fresh radium experiments are being made daily in the laboratories of the Sorbonne by Mme. Curie and her disciples, but the great secret remains unsolved. No one knows what radium is, not even in the radium factory . . . To speak of a pound of it is like speaking of a pound of sunlight . . . How great is the world's

The Standard Chemical Company not only refined radium but also made this radium solution. Customers were instructed to drink one bottle after each meal. This bottle is still radioactive more than eighty years after it was made.

demand and how limited the world's available supply may be gathered from the fact that the present price of radium is in the neighborhood of $40,000,000 a pound.

Meanwhile, in the United States, production of radium began after a source of radioactive ore was found in the Colorado Plateau. The material was mined, then shipped to a radium factory in Canonsburg, Pennsylvania. Standard Chemical Company, founded in 1911, began the slow process of producing radium, which it sold to anyone with enough money to buy it.

 # SCANDAL

Marie knew the only way to prove to the whole world that radium was a true element was to produce it in its pure metallic form. What she and Pierre had produced previously was radium salt, a powdery material made up of a high concentration of radium, yet still diluted by the presence of other elements such as sodium and chlorine. She described the process to purify radium salt into radium metal: "The method used consisted in distilling under very pure hydrogen the amalgam of radium formed by the electrolysis of a chloride solution using a mercury cathode." This time Marie was assisted in her work by André Debierne, a fellow scientist and friend of the Curies. Influenced by the Curies' discovery of radioactivity, in 1899 Debierne had discovered another new radioactive element named actinium.

The public had been interested in Marie before. But now that she was a widow with two small children to support while making her way in a scientific field of men, many were inspired by her.

Andrew Carnegie, the wealthy Pittsburgh philanthropist who built Carnegie Hall in New York City, was impressed with Marie after meeting her and wanted to help. He founded the Curie Scholarships in 1907 with $50,000, which would pay the salaries for additional staff to assist Marie in her laboratory work.

In 1910, after four years' work, Marie succeeded in purifying a tiny speck of pure radium metal, establishing without a doubt that radium was a true element. And the element radium was worth $3 million an ounce.

Lord Kelvin had been wrong; yet by the time Marie proved it, he'd been dead for three years.

Marie found that the radium metal she'd produced was unstable in its pure form. That meant that the sample she had spent four years producing had to be restored to its previous condition—radium salt, a stable form of the element.

In Marie's usual matter-of-fact way, she wrote, "So I saw at last the mysterious white metal, but could not keep it in this state, for it was required for further experiments."

Once again, at the same time Marie achieved success in her work, she experienced another heartache in her personal life. Dr. Curie, her beloved father-in-law, who had cared for her children, died. After his death, Marie hired Polish governesses for her children as she continued her work.

In January 1911, Marie's friends encouraged her to submit her name for membership to the French Academy of Sciences, the most influential scientific organization in France. A position there was open and a replacement would be elected. But a woman had never yet been allowed to become a member. Marie would be running against two men.

Marie had many friends and supporters at the Academy, but some members fought to keep the "woman" out. One man argued that "women cannot be part of the Institute of France."

On the afternoon the vote was counted, the president called the membership into the meeting by announcing, "Let everyone enter except for the women!"

When the votes were counted, Marie had lost by just one. (It would be sixty-eight more years before a woman was granted membership.) Marie never forgot, and she never again applied for a seat at the Academy. She also never again presented her scientific work to its membership.

By the end of the year, the Academy's rejection seemed like nothing compared to the trouble she found herself in.

In October 1911, while Marie attended the first Solvay Congress (a scientific meeting attended by many of the top physicists of the day) in Brussels, scandal was brewing back home. Paris newspapers were filled with rumors that Marie was having a love affair with Paul Langevin, a married man. Langevin's wife had filed for divorce and accused Marie Curie of breaking up their marriage. Madame Langevin claimed she had proof in the form of letters written by Marie to her husband.

Many people in Paris turned against Marie. Crowds gathered outside her home in Sceaux and called out "Husband-snatcher!" and "Get the foreign woman out!" For their safety, Marie and her daughters stayed with friends in Paris. Her close friends and family, including Pierre's brother, Jacques, came to support her.

Marie did not publicly admit or deny a romantic relationship with Paul Langevin. Perhaps no one but the two of them would ever know the truth. But Marie wrote a public response in a publication called *Le Temps*:

> *I find all these intrusions of the press and the public into my private life abominable . . . This is why I am going to take strong action against the publication of any documents attributed to me. Also, I have a right to demand large sums of money in reparation, and I will use this money in the interests of science.*

On November 7, 1911, in the middle of all the chaos, a telegram arrived. Marie Curie had been awarded a Nobel Prize in Chemistry for the "discovery of the elements radium and polonium, by the isolation of radium and the study of the nature and compounds of this remarkable element." It was her second Nobel Prize, and this time she alone was the recipient.

Unfortunately, even this distinction was not given as much press as the details of the scandal.

Gustave Téry, the publisher of a newspaper in Paris called *L'Oeuvre*, wrote that Marie was "an ambitious Pole who had ridden to glory on Curie's coat-tails and was now trying to latch onto Langevin's." Rumors and insults about Marie and Langevin filled Téry's newspaper. Three different duels were fought over this scandal, including one between Paul Langevin and Gustave Téry. Their weapon of choice was pistols, but when it came time to fire, neither man would shoot at the other.

While many turned their backs on Marie, a small group of her colleagues in the scientific community defended her. Marie's family encouraged her to leave France, which they believed had never given her enough credit for her work. The University of Warsaw in Poland offered her a position there. Even though Marie was publicly humiliated, she refused to be run out of France. She said, "I am French. My children are French, like Pierre. I will stay here and continue my work if I am permitted to do so."

While the scandal filled newspapers in Paris, Svante Arrhenius, a Swedish physicist and member of the Nobel committee, advised Marie not to come to accept the prize until the matter was resolved. She answered him that her work had nothing to do with her private life and that she would be accepting the prize in person.

In early December 1911, Marie took Bronya and Irène with her to Stockholm. Marie was the first person to be awarded two Nobel Prizes. This time she gave the Nobel lecture herself, explaining what she alone had accomplished and what Pierre had done.

When Marie returned from Stockholm, she collapsed from the strain of the previous months. Knowing that her private life was being discussed in newspapers tormented her. In addition to being heartsick, she was physically ill with fever and severe pain in her kidneys.

As her physical condition grew worse, the Langevins' divorce was settled on December 20, with no mention of Marie in the legal documents. At last the newspapers moved from Marie's scandal to other stories.

By the end of the year, Marie's condition was so poor that she was taken by stretcher to a clinic for treatment. She checked in under a false name.

Eve described her mother at this point in her life: "Marie had been led to the brink of suicide and of madness, and, her physical strength forsaking her, she had been brought down by a very grave illness."

She was in such poor health that she gave over control of her laboratory

In 1912, Marie was too ill to work. She was recovering from kidney surgery and public humiliation.

to her dear friend André Debierne. Marie finally had surgery on her kidneys in March 1912. She recovered for a while in the French countryside, then in England with a friend and fellow female scientist, Hertha Ayrton, known for her work with a phenomenon called the electric arc. A year passed before Marie recovered enough to return to work.

In 1913, Marie was back in her lab and wanted to keep a low profile. She felt well enough by summer to take a backpacking trip with her daughters along with her good friend Albert Einstein and his son. Yet no matter how much she wanted to keep her name out of newspapers, reporters still sought her out. While Marie attended a scientific meeting in London, a *New York Times* article from September 15, 1913, reported:

Mme. Curie shrinks from publicity to such an extent that even members of the British Association are unable to distinguish her from the ordinary women visitors at the meetings now being held here.

"Please don't write so much about me in your paper," she said to a reporter who sought an interview. "Why should you want to? Yes, I discovered radium, but you are in too much of a hurry. Wait and see what the next ten years have in store."

After the scandal surrounding Marie had faded, the Pasteur Institute joined the University of Paris in plans to build a new laboratory for France's famous professor. After all, she was the only person—not just the only woman—in the world who had won two Nobel Prizes.

The Radium Institute would be built on a street that had been named for Pierre Curie (later renamed Rue Marie et Pierre Curie). The institute would consist of two sections: one would be the Curie laboratory, where Marie would continue her research on the properties of radium and radioactivity; the other would be the Pasteur laboratory, which would study the use of radium in cancer treatment.

Marie divided her time between work in her lab on Rue Cuvier and the construction site for the Radium Institute. She planned the laboratory she and Pierre had always dreamed of having, even though it meant arguing with the architect to get every detail exactly the way she wanted it. The garden courtyard was just as important to Marie as each interior room. Long before the foundations of the buildings were poured, Marie picked out each tree that would grow there and supervised the planting. When the walls were partially constructed, Marie herself planted climbing roses that would grow up the rail of a small balcony right outside her office.

One day her old friend Petit, who had helped Marie and Pierre

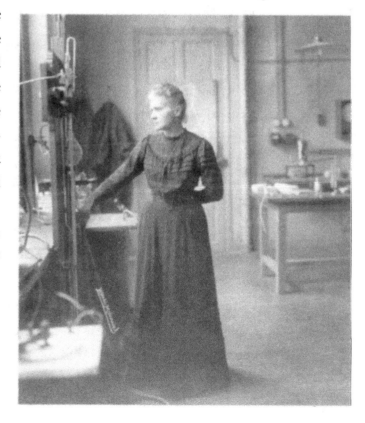

Marie Curie looking out the window of her lab on Rue Cuvier in 1913. At this time she was overseeing the building of the Radium Institute. Throughout her life, Marie never got over the bitterness she felt that Pierre had not been provided with a laboratory of his own.

The front of the Radium Institute. Today it is the home of the Curie Museum.

in their lab, came to deliver sad news to Marie. The shed where she and Pierre had discovered radium was about to be torn down to make room for new construction.

Their first lab was being demolished at the same time Marie was planning the Radium Institute. Pierre had always dreamed of working in a laboratory like those of the Radium Institute but hadn't lived to see his dream come true. Pierre was gone, and now the shed where they had shared countless hours together would be gone, too. Marie had to see it one last time.

She described her farewell:

I made my last pilgrimage there, alas, alone. On the blackboard there was still the writing of him who had been the soul of the place; the humble refuge for his research was all impregnated with his memory. The cruel reality seemed some bad dream; I almost expected to see the tall figure appear, and to hear the sound of the familiar voice.

By July 1914, the Radium Institute was finished. Marie and her lab workers moved in their few pieces of equipment. They were ready to begin their research in the new building.

But they could not do so.

WAR

World War I had begun. The German army was moving steadily through France. All of Marie's workers joined the war effort. The brand-new Radium Institute stood empty except for Marie, an old mechanic, and the cleaning woman.

While Marie was in Paris, Irène and Eve were safe in Brittany, where they'd spent the summer vacation with their governess. Fearing the Germans would overtake the city, many Parisians deserted it. The French government relocated to a safer location in Bordeaux. Marie refused to leave.

Artillery shells rained down on Paris as the

Germans approached. Marie was worried: not for her own safety but for that of her radium. To ensure its safety, Marie encased her gram of radium in lead and boarded a train to Bordeaux, where she placed it in a bank vault.

By the time she returned, the devastating Battle of the Marne had at least stopped the advance of the Germans. The war raged on, but Paris was safe. Marie allowed her daughters to return to the city.

Marie was ready to do everything she could for her adopted country's war effort. France needed money, and she was glad to give what she had by buying war bonds with her Nobel Prize money, even though she knew they might be worth nothing after the war was over. When the French government called on its citizens to donate gold, Marie offered the gold medals she'd been awarded by various scientific organizations. The official refused to take her medals.

In any event, she would not sit by and do nothing while the men of France were wounded and dying on the battlefield.

How could a scientist help?

Since the discovery of X-rays, it was possible to "see" inside the body without surgery to detect broken bones or the location of bullets. Marie understood that the ability to take X-rays of soldiers quickly after their injuries could often mean the difference between life and death. The problem was that there were few X-ray machines, and most of them were only in major hospitals. X-ray equipment needed to be closer to the battlefield.

Marie planned to change the situation.

Although she had taught and lectured about X-rays, she had never worked with them herself. First she learned how to take X-rays. Then she taught others, including seventeen-year-old Irène.

The mobile X-ray unit Marie kept for her own use from 1914 to the end of the war. She learned to drive the regulation gray Renault herself, change a flat tire, and clean the carburetor.

With the help of the Red Cross, Marie had a truck converted into a mobile X-ray unit that could drive to the patient. When she got a telegram or telephone call informing her of a battle nearby, she and a driver jumped into her equipment-filled truck and dashed off toward the hospital where the wounded had been sent. When she arrived, she prepared a room for X-ray work and was ready to examine the first patient in about thirty minutes.

Marie worked without stopping as long as any soldier needed an X-ray. Even though she could be harsh and indifferent to her own family, she showed only kindness to the soldiers she cared for. After all the soldiers who needed X-rays had been examined, Marie got back into her truck and returned to Paris.

Marie understood that each field hospital needed access to X-ray equipment and workers on a permanent basis. So she set out to provide as many as she could. After she had been called to a new battle site to use her mobile X-ray unit, she went back home and gathered together the necessary equipment to establish a permanent X-ray department. Next she found a man willing to learn how to take X-rays and trained him to do so. Then she delivered everything, worker and all, back to the field hospital to stay. Marie created two hundred permanent X-ray departments this way.

She continued working her own mobile X-ray truck as before and realized that more mobile units were needed, since they could reach remote battlefields far from a field hospital. So the more trucks they turned into mobile X-ray units, the better.

Marie knew just where to get additional vehicles. She visited rich women around Paris and convinced them to give or lend their vehicles to be converted into X-ray departments. She told the women, "I shall give you back your motor car after the war . . . If it's not useless by then, I shall give it back to you!" One by one she equipped vehicles for X-ray service. Next she had to fight the military bureaucracy to get the documents needed to clear her X-ray squadron for travel in and around the front lines.

She succeeded in equipping twenty mobile units that came to be known as "little Curies." By the end of the war, more than one million wounded men had been examined by X-ray either by one of Marie's field hospital departments or by a "little Curie."

She also saw the need to train more people to take X-rays and did so at the Radium Institute. During the last two years of the war, Marie taught 150 women how to take X-rays.

As the war continued in France, Marie had not forgotten her prized

Marie Curie and her daughter Irène working together at a field hospital in 1915. Even though she was only eighteen, Irène commanded a "little Curie" of her own. Irène received a medal for her service when the war was over.

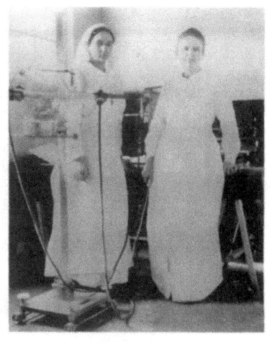

possession, which rested safely in a bank vault. In 1915 she retrieved the gram of radium she'd taken to Bordeaux. It was time to put radium to work in the war effort.

John Joly, a scientist in Dublin, Ireland, had developed a method of collecting radon gas in tiny glass tubes. Since radon's half-life was less than four days, it was safer to handle and transport than radium, yet like radium it could be used to treat cancers and skin conditions. Once a week, Marie collected radon from her radium and sent the tubes out to local hospitals.

Radium helped the war effort in a totally different way as well. Its ability to glow in the dark was used to advantage when a radium-based paint was developed that could be used on the dials of soldiers' wristwatches, airplane instruments, and gun sights. A whole new industry using radium was created to provide these products, which would later have serious consequences.

In the fall of 1918, the war was over. As Marie suspected they would be, the war bonds she had bought with her Nobel money were worthless now. She was poor—again.

But with the end of the war, Marie's beloved Poland was free at last. Pol-

This crucifix used radium to glow in the dark. The ad says, "The price is low enough so *every catholic family should own one."*

ish children no longer had to learn their native language in secret, or be forced to admit that a foreign power ruled over them, as Marie had. Marie wrote that the Polish dream of freedom "that appeared so difficult to realize, although so dear, became a reality following the storm that swept over Europe."

When the Radium Institute officially opened its doors after the war, it had little equipment and few workers. Marie concentrated once again on making the laboratory she and Pierre had always wanted. Her job as director took up much of her time, but, as always, she continued her own research.

She taught a class in the Institute's amphitheater on Monday and Wednesday afternoons. On Tuesday and Friday mornings, the world-

Even in the late 1940s and early 1950s, kids could order this "Atomic 'Bomb' " ring for fifteen cents and a box top from Kix breakfast cereal. The ad said you could "see genuine atoms split to smithereens!" To see this wonderful sight, you had to go into a dark room, allow your eyes to adjust to the darkness, take the tail fin off the ring, and look inside the aluminum end. You could see tiny flashes of light come and go as individual atoms of a radioactive material gave off energy and lit up the zinc sulfide in the ring. The ad guaranteed the ring was safe and the material inside was harmless. (Radium was not used, but polonium may have been.) This was a toy version of an instrument used by scientists to detect radioactivity called a spinthariscope.

famous scientist gave interviews to the press, who flocked to Paris to speak to her. Reporters were told before their interviews that Madame Curie would speak to them only about technical things; she would not discuss personal issues at all.

One of these interviews would change her life.

Missy Meloney, an American magazine reporter, had been trying to get an interview with Madame Curie for years. She finally got to meet with her in May 1920. She described her first meeting with Marie:

> *I saw a pale, timid little woman in a black cotton dress, with the saddest face I had ever looked upon.*
>
> *Her well-formed hands were rough. I noticed a characteristic, nervous little habit of rubbing the tips of her fingers over the pad of her thumb in quick succession. I learned later that working with radium had made them numb.*

During the interview, Marie named the location of each of the fifty grams of radium that were in America. When Missy asked how much radium was in France, she was surprised at the answer. In all of France there was only one gram of radium, the one produced by Marie and Pierre.

"*You* have only a gram?" Missy asked.

"I? Oh, I have none," Marie corrected her. "It belongs to my laboratory."

Missy was shocked. The woman who had first discovered and produced radium had given it to the Radium Institute. Missy had expected to find Marie a wealthy woman, but instead she found a woman who was barely surviving on her professor's salary. She noticed that the Radium Institute was badly furnished and had little equipment compared with sophisticated laboratories such as Thomas Edison's in America.

She asked Marie about patents on radium that would have made the Curies rich.

"There were no patents. We were working in the interests of science. Radium was not to enrich any one. Radium is an element. It belongs to all people," Marie answered.

"What would you like to possess most?" Missy asked.

"I need a gram of radium to continue my researches, but I cannot buy it: radium is too dear for me."

At the time, a gram of radium cost $100,000.

The injustice of Marie's situation outraged Missy Meloney. While others around the world were making money from radium, Marie Curie couldn't afford to buy any of the element she had discovered. Missy determined to do something about it.

Back in New York, she devised a plan. She would organize a drive to collect the $100,000 needed to buy Marie Curie a gram of radium. And she would ask American women to make the donations.

In less than a year, Missy had collected around $150,000 from American

Marie Curie surrounded by photographers after arriving in New York in 1921. Irène, Eve, and Missy Meloney (facing Marie) are standing to Marie's right. So many admirers shook Marie's hand that it injured her arm, requiring her to wear a sling. They sailed to America on the SS *Olympic*, a sister ship of the SS *Titanic*.

women to buy radium for Marie. Some donors were people who had previously been cured of cancer through radium treatments.

Missy invited Marie and her daughters to come to America to accept the gift of radium, which had been produced in the United States by the Standard Chemical Company. When their ship docked in New York, Marie was overwhelmed by the crowd who'd gathered to greet her. Reporters, Girl Scouts, schoolgirls, women from Polish organizations, and others welcomed the famous scientist.

Marie, Irène, and Eve were swept up in an exhausting swirl of activities. Marie was showered with honors and awards everywhere she went. On May 20, 1921, Warren Harding, the President of the United States, presented Marie with two symbols of the gift of radium: one was a legal document of ownership (Marie insisted the radium be given to the Radium Institute rather than to her personally), the other a small gold key on a silk cord that he placed around her neck. The key fit a wooden box that had been built to transport the radium back to France. In addition to radium, Marie was given other gifts, including equipment, cash awards from different groups, and valuable radioactive materials such as mesothorium, a decay product of the element thorium. Marie wore the same black dress she had worn years before when she accepted both Nobel Prizes.

Marie didn't feel well during her visit to America and decided to cut her trip short. While Missy Meloney had been collecting money in America for the Marie Curie Radium Campaign, Marie began having problems with her eyesight. Both of Marie's eyes had cataracts (a condition in which the lens becomes cloudy). It's likely that the cause was Marie's work with radium and her repeated exposure to X-rays during the war.

In a letter to Bronya on November 20, 1920, Marie had written:

My greatest troubles come from my eyes and ears. My eyes have grown much weaker, and probably very little can be done about them. As for the ears, an

almost continuous humming, sometimes very intense, persecutes me. I am very worried about it: my work may be interfered with—or even become impossible. Perhaps radium has something to do with these troubles, but it cannot be affirmed with certainty.

These are my troubles. Don't speak of them to anybody.

Marie working in her private lab in 1921. Today it is part of the Curie Museum. Before the public could tour it, the room had to be decontaminated of radioactivity.

This is the first indication that Marie considered that radium might be the cause of her health problems.

She visited a doctor in New York about her eyesight before she returned home. After she had sailed, a *Times* article on July 1, 1921, reported a doctor in New York had confirmed that Marie Curie was "threatened with blindness." The article also said that the scientist's friends "denied that her eyes were affected," and that she went to the doctor to "have her glasses repaired."

Back in France, Marie's vision continually grew worse. Afraid of publicity, she didn't want anyone to know. She kept up the pretense that nothing was wrong with her eyesight. And everyone close to her helped her pretend. When she searched for the salt shaker at the dinner table, her daughters handed it to her. When she crossed the street, her daughters took her arm to guide her. In her lab, she posted colored signs on her equipment. When she taught class, she wrote her lecture notes in huge letters. Marie wouldn't allow failing eyesight to slow her down.

Around this time, Missy Meloney, who had become a good friend to Marie, persuaded Marie to write about herself, Pierre, and their work together. During the time when her eyesight was poor, Marie nevertheless wrote a book that she entitled *Pierre Curie*, published in 1923. Even though she rarely was willing to talk about Pierre, in this book Marie lovingly wrote of his early life and their work on radium. It was only at Missy's insistence that Marie wrote her brief autobiographical notes, which appeared in the back. Perhaps the most personal passage is in the section where Marie describes Pierre's death:

In 1906 just as we were definitely giving up the old shed laboratory where we had been so happy, there came the dreadful catastrophe which took my husband away from me and left me alone to bring up our children and, at the same time, to continue our work of research. It is impossible for me to express the profoundness and importance of the crisis brought into my life by the loss of the one who had been my closest companion and best friend. Crushed by the blow, I did not feel able to face the future. I could not forget, however, what my husband used sometimes to say, that, even deprived of him, I ought to continue my work.

With the book completed, Marie finally agreed to have cataract surgery in 1923. Once again she used a false name to protect her privacy. More surgery was needed in 1924 and again in 1930. Eventually, with the help of thick glasses and determination, Marie was able to see well enough to work again. In a letter to Bronya in September 1927, she wrote:

Sometimes my courage fails me and I think I ought to stop working, live in the country and devote myself to gardening. But I am held by a thousand bonds, and I don't know when I shall be able to arrange things otherwise. Nor do I know whether, even by writing scientific books, I could live without the laboratory.

DANGER

As more and more radium was being produced around the world, the price went down. Although it was still expensive, some doctors bought their own supply to use in their medical practices. Several major cities in the world established "radium banks" that rented out radium to doctors for a day or two.

Newspapers ran success stories of cancer patients, like the seventeen-year-old girl with a beautiful singing voice who'd had a tumor removed from her left vocal cord. The tumor grew back and was removed again. The next time the tumor grew back, she could speak only in a whisper. Two months after she underwent radium therapy, the tumor was gone and her singing voice had returned.

After using radium to treat cancer with success, some doctors began using it for non-life-threatening conditions such as high blood pressure, acne, ulcers, diabetes, infected wounds, and various skin problems. Patients, including children, were injected with radium by their doctors, who thought the radium would help them from within. Authors Jack Shubert and Ralph E. Lapp wrote in their book *Radiation: What It Is and How It Affects You* that one physician had given more than seven thousand injections of radium to his patients.

The general public believed radium was good for one's health and that it could cure almost any physical problem. A new fad swept through Paris called "Radium Tea." From three to five o'clock, society women gathered at a local establishment to drink tea, talk, and play cards or read, while oxygen that had passed through a container of radium circulated around the room. The doctor in charge claimed that if they spent two hours there daily for a month, it

The same principle behind Radium Tea continues today in deserted uranium mines in Montana. Even after mining, the natural radium in the ground constantly gives off radon. Since the 1950s, people have paid to sit in the underground mines to expose themselves to radon, believing it cures their physical problems. Couches, chairs, and tables are provided as well as heat lamps to keep away the chill of the constant 58-to-60-degree temperature.

would cure the women of "rheumatism or, in general, of all [afflictions] of the heart or bone joints."

When products containing radium were made available, people bought them without hesitation. Radium was used in some medications, toothpaste, bathing powder, radioactive pads similar to heating pads, glow-in-the-dark buttons, plant fertilizer, soap, and fishing lures.

The word *radium* or anything similar to it caught the attention of the buying public. And some products that claimed to contain radium didn't have any in them at all. One such product was Radol, sold as a cancer treatment by a man who called himself Dr. Rupert Wells. In reality, he was not a doctor at all; he was Dennis Rupert Dupuis. Around 1908, he sold more than seven thousand bottles

250 Radium Eclipse Sprayers
Absolutely Free

With Every Gallon Can ($2.50) of Radium Cleanse

Radium Chemical Co.

This ad offers a free insect sprayer with the purchase of a $2.50 gallon of Radium Cleanser, which it claimed killed all types of insects and had "no equal as a cleaner of Furniture, Paintwork, Porcelain, Tile, etc."

of Radol at $15 for a month's worth. "Dr. Wells" claimed his radium elixir, Radol, could "cure cancer at home without pain, plaster or operation. I have discovered a new and seemingly unfailing remedy for the deadly cancer. I have made some most astonishing cures. My marvelous radiotized fluid did it." When a government agency found that Radol did not contain any radium at all, Dupuis was put out of business.

Marie Curie, of course, had nothing at all to do with any of these prod-

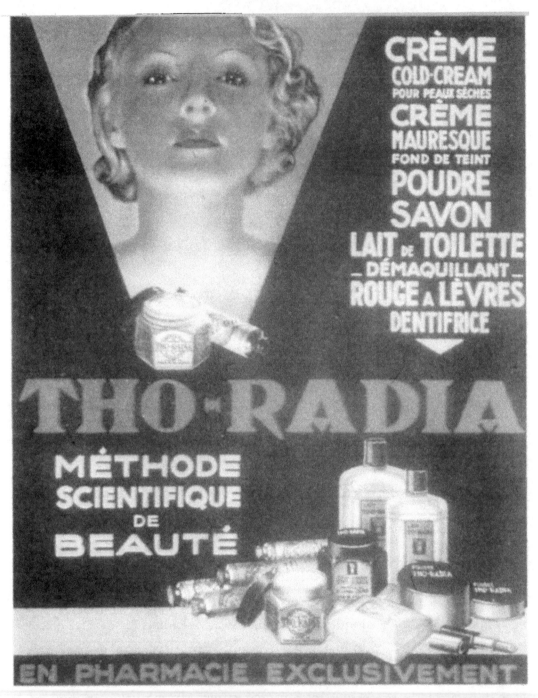

In France, Tho-radia beauty products claimed to contain radium and thorium and to have been developed by Dr. Alfred Curie. Although the name sounded familiar to the buying public, no one by that name was related to Pierre Curie. According to *Living with Radiation: The First Hundred Years* by Frame and Kolb, in 1980, when these products were tested, they did not contain any radium or thorium at all.

ucts. Eve described her mother as being "exasperated and helpless" over the way people were exploiting radium. Marie continually refused to profit from it, even while others were getting rich.

It seemed radium could do no wrong. But suddenly radium's reputation began to tarnish.

"New Radium Disease Found; Has Killed 5" was the headline on a May 30, 1925, article in *The New York Times*. The story reported that "five women have died, and ten others have been stricken with a new disease believed to be 'radium necrosis,' because of infection received while painting watch dials with a radium preparation in a factory in East Orange, N. J."

During World War I, a number of women and girls, some as young as twelve years old, had been hired by the Radium Luminous Materials Corporation (later U.S. Radium Corp.) to paint the hands and numbers on the dials of wristwatches with radium paint so they would glow in the dark. Painting watch dials at the factory in New Jersey was considered a good job for young women, many of whom were from immigrant families. The pay, at $20 per week, was more than they could make most other places. Also, it was exciting to work with the world-famous radium.

Each worker mixed dry radium paint powder with zinc sulfide and paint thinner to complete between 250 and 300 watch-dial faces per day. The watch faces were small, so a brush with a sharp tip was necessary to paint the tiny numbers. To keep a point on the brush, the women would put the brush between their lips before dipping it into the paint. Over and over throughout each day, the women lip-pointed their gritty, tasteless brushes. By the end of the workday, the dial painters were covered with radium paint dust.

For laughs, some girls decorated their buttons or belts with radium

Jewelers used these touch-up kits for radium dials. By 1919, more than two million radium dials had been manufactured. Dial painters coated the watch hands with radium-based paint mixed with zinc sulfide. The radium reacted with the zinc to produce a glow brighter than radium could alone, making the tiny watch hands visible in the dark. But over time, even though the radium lost none of its strength, it destroyed the zinc. A jeweler could touch up the dial face with one of these kits.

paint, and others painted their fingernails or teeth to show their boyfriends how they could glow in the dark.

The company assured the girls that the radium paint was harmless. It wasn't. Each time they tipped their brushes in their mouths, they ingested tiny amounts of radium that were absorbed by their bones, teeth, and organs and irradiated their entire bodies.

Amelia Maggia and her four sisters painted dials at the factory. In 1921, Amelia began having problems. Her cheek was swollen, and she had a severe toothache. She had her tooth pulled, but the empty tooth socket would not heal. Infection set in and rotted her jawbone so badly that, according to Claudia Clark's *Radium Girls*, "her dentist lifted her entire mandible [lower jaw] out of her mouth."

Amelia died in 1922. No one suspected it could have had anything to do with her job.

Later that year, however, another dial painter developed symptoms just like Amelia's: a swollen cheek, a severe toothache that required pulling the tooth, the empty tooth socket that wouldn't heal, rotting bone and flesh, and fatigue caused by severe anemia (a condition in which the number

Young women working at a factory painting watch dials. Many dial painters died a slow, miserable death from radium poisoning.

of red blood cells, which transport oxygen throughout the body, is below normal).

Then another dial painter developed the same symptoms, and another.

Dr. Walter Barry, a local oral surgeon, treated these young women who had similar mysterious conditions. They had one more thing in common: each had worked as a dial painter.

Throughout 1925, newspapers reported stories of dial painters who were sick and dying. The U.S. Department of Labor ordered an investigation into radium paint factories to find out if radium was the cause.

On June 21, 1925, the *Times* reported the situation of two sisters who had been dial painters. Sarah Maillefer had died from what her family claimed was "radium poisoning," and her sister, Marguerite Carlough, was

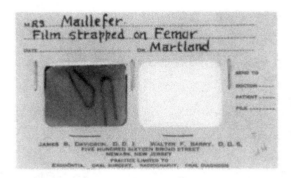

MR9 Maillefer
Film strapped on Femur
Dr. Martland

JAMES B. DAVIDSON, D.D.S   WALTER F. BARRY, D.D.S.
FIVE HUNDRED SIXTEEN BROAD STREET
NEWARK, NEW JERSEY
PRACTICE LIMITED TO
ENDODONTIA, ORAL SURGERY, RADIOGRAPHY, ORAL DIAGNOSIS

This image was taken of Sarah Maillefer's leg bone after her death. Two metal clips were placed between the bone and an X-ray film for six weeks. The radiation emitted from her leg bone made the image. The clips can be clearly seen.

close to death. The same article said, "C. B. Lee, Treasurer of the company [U.S. Radium Corp.], said yesterday that company officials do not believe that any of the deaths were caused by conditions in the factory . . . Radium in the infinitesimal quantities used in the dial paint was helpful rather than injurious to the human system."

More and more young women who had been dial painters fell victim to the strange disease. The battle raged over whether radium was the cause of their problems.

In 1928, five women banded together to sue their former employer, U.S. Radium Corp.: Edna Hussman, Katherine Schaub, Grace Fryer, Quinta McDonald, and Albina Larice. (McDonald and Larice were sisters of Amelia Maggia, the first dial painter to die.) These women became known as the Radium Girls.

Each of them asked for $250,000 in damages. Although they were not the first dial painters to sue the company, theirs would be the first case to be tried in court.

But by the time their case got to court, the women were very sick. The two sisters were bedridden. Grace Fryer couldn't walk and had to wear a back brace to sit up. All five were so weak that they couldn't raise their arms to take an oath in court.

The public sympathized with the Radium Girls as doctors testified they were suffering from a condition "for which there was no remedy known to

Five Women, Facing Death By Radium Poisoning, Plead For Justice While They Liv

MISS KATHERINE SCHAUB

MRS. ALBINA LARICE

MRS. EDNA HUSSMAN

HOW RADIUM KILLS

Radio activity within the body is described by Dr. Robert E. Humphries, chief surgeon of the New Jersey Orthopedic Hospital in Orange, as the slow burning up of the human frame. The radio active particles which are taken into the body attack the bones in every part of the skeleton and it is believed that the rotting of the bones, a very slow process, is the reason that the disease is unperceived by the victim for a period ranging from two to four years after infection. In some cases the first indication has come in a painful tooth. In others the bones of the legs are affected, causing a shortening of a limb. Even the skull does not escape the scourge.

the hearing which will determine

The Radium Girls (clockwise from top): Katherine Schaub, Albina Larice, Edna Hussman, Grace Fryer, and Quinta McDonald. They didn't realize that each time they pointed their brushes in their mouths as they painted watch dials, they were swallowing tiny amounts of radium. Their breath was so radioactive that if they breathed on a fluorescent screen, it would light up. Grace Fryer said that when she blew her nose, her handkerchief glowed in the dark.

science and were facing almost certain death." Clark's book quotes twenty-six-year-old Katherine Schaub: "While other girls are going to dances and the theater and courting and marrying for love I have to remain here and watch painful death approach."

It was reported that Marie Curie suggested the women could eat raw liver to help fight against the severe anemia. *The New York Journal* on May 26, 1926, quoted Marie, however, as saying, "There is absolutely no means of destroying the substance once it enters the human body." The type of radium exposure the Radium Girls received was different from Marie's. The dial painters had swallowed radium, which was absorbed by their bodies. They were continuously being irradiated by radium from inside. Marie's exposure was primarily external and her direct contact with it less frequent.

U.S. Radium Corp. decided to settle with the women out of court on June 4, 1928. Each woman received ten thousand dollars, plus six hundred dollars per year during her lifetime, and her medical bills would be paid by the company.

Through the late 1920s and early 1930s, each Radium Girl died a slow and agonizing death.

The watch dials they painted continued to glow in the dark.

Even as the tragic news of the dial painters filled the newspapers in America, the official position of the Radium Institute about the dangers of radium was that if radium posed any health risk at all, it was a small one.

Elizabeth Rona, a nuclear scientist who worked at the Institute for a time and later in America, wrote about Marie Curie in her book *How It Came About: Radioactivity, Nuclear Physics, Atomic Energy*. "Each time there was a dangerous experiment, she carried it out herself," she wrote. About the laboratory she said, "The Curie Institute was highly contaminated. The staff was more concerned with the safety of the radium sources than with their own."

Marie insisted her staff abide by a few basic safety precautions: since radiation does not penetrate lead easily, they were to protect themselves with lead shielding as much as possible, and they were not to use their bare hands to handle tubes containing radium. But Marie herself ignored even these precautions; her blood count had been abnormal for years.

Marie's advice to all who worked at the Radium Institute was to breathe deeply while outdoors. When three lab workers died of either anemia or

Several companies produced radium pads that were designed to be placed on any painful body part, like a heating pad without the cord. The pad that came in this box had selling points that set it apart from the competition. First, the Radiumchema pad assured its customers that the radioactive products it contained were the only ones authorized by the state of St. Joachimsthal, which was the source of the Curies' original pitchblende. Next, on the back of the box was a certificate from the Curie Laboratory/Radium Institute guaranteeing that the pad actually contained radium. It was signed by Sonia Cotelle, a Polish radiochemist who worked with Marie Curie. Sadly, Cotelle died from radiation overexposure after she accidentally swallowed polonium during an experiment.

Marie in her office at the Radium Institute in 1928. Her personal laboratory was in the next room.

leukemia, she would not accept the possibility that radium was the cause. She believed it was because they didn't get enough fresh air.

No one knows why Marie, who had worked with radium longer than anyone, was still alive while others around her were dying from its effects. Perhaps her lifelong habits of swimming, bicycling, and hiking made her physically strong enough to counteract the poisoning. But she was by no means in good health. At this point, besides poor vision, numb fingertips, and the humming in her ears, she was constantly tired.

Despite her problems, Marie kept complete control over everything that happened at the Radium Institute. She supervised twenty to thirty workers, including her daughter Irène, who, as Marie's assistant, continued research on radioactive substances. Marie also taught two classes a week, which left little time for her own research.

Marie wanted Poland to have access to a radium cancer treatment and research center like the one in France. She enlisted Bronya's help to oversee building a radium institute in Warsaw. Bronya launched a campaign that encouraged people to buy just one brick for the Marie Sklodowska-Curie Institute. When enough bricks and funds were available to begin construction, Marie went to Warsaw for the ceremony to mark the occasion. In the presence of the President, the mayor, and other dignitaries, Marie spoke Polish publicly in a free Poland.

As the construction neared completion, there wasn't enough money to buy a gram of radium to use for cancer therapy. One more time Marie's old friend Missy Meloney came to the rescue. Missy organized and collected money from the American public again to buy the now-$50,000 gram of radium for the new Marie Sklodowska-Curie Institute in Warsaw. Marie again agreed to come to the United States to accept the gift.

In October 1929, Americans welcomed Marie with the same enthusiasm they had eight years before. She was invited by Henry Ford, founder of Ford Motor Company, to attend the golden jubilee celebration of the invention of electric light to honor the inventor, Thomas Edison. The President of the United States, Herbert Hoover, made the presentation to Marie at the White House. This time the gift was not actually radium but the money with which to buy it.

The timing of the fund-raising was fortunate, for a few days later America was in financial turmoil. The stock market crashed on October 24, 1929, also known as "Black Thursday." Many wealthy people lost all their money on that day. It was the start of the Great Depression.

Back home in Paris, Marie once again settled into her routine of teaching and working. The year after her trip to the United States, she participated in a League of Nations committee on intellectual cooperation in Geneva. One of the highlights for Marie was to spend time with her old friend Albert Einstein. An article in *The New York Times* on July 27, 1930, described the reaction of the crowd as they watched the two famous scientists talking together: "People simply stand at a respectful distance and stare, or tiptoe by these friends who knew each other before either was known to the world."

Though she had been famous for many years, the public was still fascinated by Marie. Requests for autographs and photographs constantly poured in. To each request a card was sent that read, "Mme Curie does not wish to give autographs or sign photographs and asks you to excuse her."

One autograph seeker in England thought he had found a way to get her signature. He sent a check made out to Marie Curie, asking her to cash it and donate the money to her favorite charity. In this way, when she en-

Marie Curie and Albert Einstein. These two famous scientists met at the Solvay Congress of 1911 and had great admiration for each other. They remained close friends through the years. Einstein said, "Marie Curie is, of all celebrated beings, the only one whom fame has not corrupted."

Degnen's Radio-Active Solar Pad sold for $19.50 in the 1920s. The company claimed the pad would relieve high blood pressure, stimulate blood circulation, help overcome diseases, and relieve indigestion, rheumatism, nervous headaches, and more. One customer claimed the Radio-Active Solar Pad cured her cancer. The company information also said that with this pad "it is not an idle dream to look forward to the time when Radium will furnish all of the light, heat and power necessary for the human race."

dorsed the check on the back, the man would have her autograph on the canceled check. Marie was not fooled. The check was returned to him—unsigned.

In 1932, Marie's health was further failing. She sometimes stayed in bed for days at a time but went back to her classroom and duties at the Institute as soon as possible. On days she went to work, a chauffeur-driven Ford automobile that Henry Ford had given her as a personal gift honked for her at about 8:45 a.m. When she came home from the laboratory, sometimes as late as eight o'clock, her daughter Eve described her mother as having a "face quite pale, worn and aged by fatigue." Marie would say to Eve, "Ah! How tired I am!"

Pushing through her weariness, Marie completed another goal. The Marie Sklodowska-Curie Institute in Warsaw was dedicated on May 29, 1932. In a letter to Eve from Poland, Marie wrote about the beauty of the Vistula River, saying it "winds lazily along its wide bed, bluish green near at hand but made bluer far off by the reflection of the sky . . . The river has a profound attraction for me, the origins of which I do not know." It was to be the last time Marie saw her beloved Poland.

As Marie's fatigue was getting harder and harder to ignore, disturbing news about radium filled American newspapers: it had killed again.

"Death Stirs Action on Radium 'Cures'" was the headline in *The New York Times* on April 2, 1932. The article reported the death of Eben Byers, a well-known American millionaire and amateur golfer. Byers had died from radium poisoning.

In 1927, Byers was returning home by train from a Harvard-Yale football game when he fell out of the upper berth and hurt his arm. When the pain from his injury didn't go away and began to interfere with his golf game, his doctor suggested a new "radium cure" called Radithor.

Radithor, water laced with radium and mesothorium, had been created by William J. A. Bailey. Beginning in the mid-1920s, Bailey created four different companies that sold radium products. Some contained radium; some didn't. One of his products that did was called Arium tablets. They cost one dollar for "Forty-two Tablets of Genuine Radium." But the Department of Agriculture ordered Bailey's products to be removed from the market and destroyed because some didn't contain radium as advertised. This time Bailey made sure his new product, Radithor, contained what he claimed.

Radithor was different from radium water made in crocks. Water from crocks became

Radithor was the deadliest of all radium water products sold to the public because it contained the highest dose of radium. Bailey Radium Laboratories guaranteed that "Radithor is harmless in every respect." Each bottle cost one dollar, and at least 400,000 bottles were sold. Radithor also offered a one-thousand-dollar award to anyone who could prove that it "does not contain a definite amount of both Radium and Mesothorium elements."

slightly radioactive after being exposed to radon. With Radithor, users consumed actual radium.

Company product information claimed Radithor could treat sixty-eight different conditions, from heart disease to obesity. Bailey described it as "perpetual sunshine" and said, "By merely drinking Radithor, the radioactive elements are distributed throughout the whole body where they shower their billions of rays on the cells to stimulate their function."

When Eben Byers started drinking several bottles of Radithor each day in 1927, his arm felt much better. As a matter of fact, his whole body felt invigorated. He was so impressed with it that he bought cases of the expensive elixir to give his friends. He even gave it to his racehorses. For about two years, during the time when news of the Radium Girls filled newspapers, Byers drank more than one thousand bottles of Radithor.

By early 1930, Byers didn't feel invigorated anymore. He'd lost weight and suffered from headaches and toothaches. Then his teeth started falling out. Doctors discovered that holes were forming in his skull and his bones were rotting away, just as had happened to the Radium Girls. Radium had collected in his bones and organs and was slowly killing him.

When Eben Byers died on March 31, 1932, the former athlete weighed ninety-two pounds. His autopsy proved he died from radium poisoning. His bones were even more radioactive than those of the Radium Girls.

An article in the July 1932 issue of *Popular Science Monthly* reported:

Byers' body contained the largest amount of radium ever found in a human being—more than thirty micrograms, enough to kill three men. One microgram is one millionth of a gram, and it takes more than twenty-eight grams to make one ounce.

You will understand how infinitesimal a quantity ten micrograms is when you realize that a grain of sand weighs about one milligram, or one thou-sandth of a gram. If the sand grain were split up into one hundred particles, each one would be the size of a lethal dose of radium.

By the time of Byers' death, Radithor had been under investigation for about two years. On April 3, 1932, the *Times* reported that the assistant chief of the Food and Drug Administration, Paul Dunbar, was

prompted by the death of Mr. Byers to warn the public against the indiscrim-inate use of radium preparations without proper medical advice . . .

"We were afraid something like this would happen," [Dunbar said.] "In 1928 we made a survey of the many radium products on the market and be-gan issuing warnings to the public . . . I feel that any preparation contain-ing radium is a pretty dangerous thing."

The same article said the city health officer of Newark, New Jersey, sent

inspectors out to locate and "stop the sale of any patent medicine of a radioactive nature and [said] that they would seize any radium water or patent medicine of that nature found in any drug stores in Newark."

It seems the death of a wealthy American man caused more con-

Radium suppositories for those who wanted to approach medicine from all directions.

cern over radium overexposure than the deaths of the many poor women who had been dial painters.

Around this time Dr. E. E. Free, a teacher at New York University, gave a demonstration of radium poisoning using a Geiger counter (a device that detects and measures radiation) on the bones of an unnamed victim. It was broadcast on the radio by the Columbia Broadcasting System (CBS). An article in *The New York Times* on May 1, 1932, reported Dr. Free's explanation of what happens when radium accumulates in the bones of people: "It begins shooting out atomic particles. Gradually this bombardment of the bones from traitor atoms admitted inside them, causes damage so that the victim of this radium poisoning dies." Next he connected a Geiger counter to a loudspeaker so the audience could hear the click of the counter as it detected radioactivity. The article noted that "the sound of radium rays coming from the bones of victims of radium poisoning sounded like peas being dropped slowly into a pan."

The dangers associated with radium were often reported in newspapers, yet companies continued to use radium in their products. And the public continued to buy them.

The Lifestone Cigarette Holder supposedly protected "your health from injurious" elements in cigarettes as the smoke passed through a radium source. It also promised beautiful faces and excellent health.

ENDINGS

By 1934, Marie had developed gallstones. Eve wrote that her mother often talked of her own death, saying, "I am worried about the fate of the Institute of Radium when I am no longer there." As the end of her mother's life approached, Eve described Marie's attitude: "There was no serenity, no acceptance, in her. She repulsed with all her instinct the idea of an end."

Eve believed her mother "made a point of proving to herself that she was not in poor health. She went skating at Versailles, and joined

Irène in the ski fields of Savoy." And when Bronya visited Marie, she "organized a motoring trip in the south."

Marie and Bronya took the trip they'd planned, but Marie was exhausted and had caught a cold by the time she returned home. Entering the house, Marie, "shaken by a chill, suddenly abandoned herself to an attack of despair. She sobbed in Bronya's arms like a sick child."

Throughout her life, Marie appeared to the world as if she had everything under control, that she was tough, that she could do it all alone. Only her trusted sister Bronya was allowed to see her vulnerable side. The sisters had an unbreakable bond. They'd helped each other get an education many years before and continued to encourage and comfort each other through life's problems.

By the next morning, Marie was back to her old self again.

A few days later, the sisters said goodbye at the train station when Bronya returned to Poland. They would not see each other again.

Marie went to the Institute almost every day even though she constantly had fever, fatigue, and violent chills. One afternoon in May she said, "I have a fever, and I must go home." On her way out of the courtyard, Marie admired the flowers that were coming up and noticed that one of the climbing roses outside her office needed some attention. She called to her me-

Marie Curie on the terrace outside her laboratory at the Radium Institute. This photo was taken just months before her death. The climbing roses she planted are in the foreground. Marie's roses still grow there today.

chanic and said, "Georges, look at this rose vine: you must see to it right away!"

It was the last time she would see her beloved Radium Institute.

Her doctors were called but, as usual, could find nothing in particular wrong with Marie. They wondered if she might have tuberculosis lesions in her lungs and suggested she go to a sanatorium in the mountains (a common treatment of the day).

The trip was difficult for Marie since she was so sick. At the sanatorium, X-rays of her lungs indicated she did not have tuberculosis. The trip to the mountains didn't help her.

Marie's fever shot up to 104 degrees Fahrenheit. According to Eve, "She hardly spoke by then, but her paling eyes reflected a great fear." After more blood tests, the doctor announced a diagnosis: aplastic pernicious anemia (a severe blood disease), which he believed was caused by overexposure to radiation.

As Marie was teetering between life and death, her mind went back to the place she loved best, the laboratory. Lost in the past, she mumbled, "Was it done with radium or with mesothorium?"

Marie Sklodowska Curie died on July 4, 1934, at the age of sixty-six.

On July 6, Marie's body was buried in the country cemetery in Sceaux. Her plain oak coffin was placed on top of Pierre's. Just as Marie would have wanted it, there were no religious officials or state officials, only family, close friends, and co-workers in attendance. Hundreds of birds sang in a nearby tree as each mourner walked by her coffin and placed a rose on it.

The climbing rose Marie had planted at Pierre's grave twenty-eight years earlier was in full bloom.

Joseph and Bronya, Marie's brother and sister, each brought Marie one last gift. Upon her coffin they scattered a handful of earth—from Poland.

———

In 1995, the French government honored Marie and Pierre Curie once again. They moved their remains from the small cemetery in Sceaux to the Pantheon, where some of France's most famous dead are laid to rest.

Marie Sklodowska Curie, still breaking records years after her death, was the first woman to be given this honor on her own merit.

LEGACY

The life of Marie Curie demonstrates that one person can make a difference in the world. She overcame obstacles of poverty, fear, depression, discrimination, personal grief, and public humiliation to accomplish groundbreaking scientific work.

Marie's work on radium opened the door to the nuclear age in which we live. Perhaps even more important than radium was her breakthrough discovery that radioactivity is an atomic process. It is this atomic nature of radioactivity that makes nuclear energy possible, as well as radiocarbon dating (a method for determining the age of some organic material by measuring the amount of radioactive carbon).

Marie devoted her life's work to radium, yet it is not used commercially today. It has been replaced by other radioactive elements, including artificial radioactivity, which was discovered by her daughter Irène and her husband, Frédéric Joliot, for which they shared a Nobel Prize in Chemistry in 1935.

Today radioactivity has been put to use in many different ways. Nuclear energy powers electricity plants, navy submarines and ships, spacecraft in deep space, and pacemakers. Radioactive elements are used in the health field to treat cancer, to conduct various laboratory tests, to sterilize medical supplies, and to diagnose diseases using nuclear medicine images. In other industries, radioactive materials are used to irradiate food to destroy bacteria and pests, to test the density of road surfaces, to locate gas and mineral deposits, and to check welds on industrial equipment. Tiny amounts of radioactive elements are used in consumer products such as smoke detectors, starters for fluorescent lights, mantles of gas camping lamps, and welding rods.

Marie Curie's legacy of radioactivity has been both a benefit and a detriment to humanity. While the proper use of cancer therapy has saved many lives, the misuse of radioactivity has taken lives through the years.

One person *can* change the world.

SOURCE NOTES

The most helpful primary sources used in the writing of this book were:

Eve Curie. *Madame Curie: A Biography*. Trans. by Vincent Sheean. Garden City, N.Y.: Doubleday, 1937.

Marie Curie. *Pierre Curie*. Trans. by Charlotte and Vernon Kellogg. New York: Macmillan, 1923.

To simplify the following notes, *Madame Curie: A Biography* is abbreviated *MC*; *Pierre Curie* is abbreviated *PC*.

BEGINNINGS

4–8 *"Please call"*; *"Manya Sklodowska"*; *"Your prayer"*; *"Our Father"*; *"Who rules"*; *"restore our mother's"*; *"That's stupid!"*: *MC*, 19, 17, 20, 20, 21, 9, 27.

9 *"Constantly held"*: *PC*, 159.

9–10 *"It's my brother"*; *"To the Poles"*: *MC*, 38, 37.

10 *"nervous troubles"*: Rosalynd Pflaum, *Grand Obsession: Marie Curie and Her World* (New York: Doubleday, 1989), 10.

10 *"The fatigue"*: *PC*, 163.

GOVERNESS

12 *"My existence"*: *MC*, 60.

13 *"My heart was heavy"*: *PC*, 163.

13 *"I have made friends"*: MC, 64.

14 *"even this innocent work"*: PC, 165.

14 *"At nine"*: MC, 72.

14 *"acquired the habit"*: PC, 166.

15–18 *"My plans"*; *"now that I have lost"*; *"afraid for myself"*; *"If you only knew"*; *"Everybody says"*; *"And now you, my little Manya"*; *"I have been stupid"*: MC, 72, 75, 77, 78, 80, 83–84, 84.

19 *"To my great joy"*: PC, 167.

19 *"I ask you"*; *"not be away long"*: MC, 88, 90.

PIERRE

21 *"All that I saw"*: PC, 171.

21 *"had the habit"*: MC, 106.

22–23 *"It was not unusual"*; *"were often reduced"*; *"the heroic period"*; *"It would be impossible"*: PC, 170, 170, 172–73, 170–73.

24 *"very satisfied"*: MC, 115.

25–27 *"Upon entering"*; *"dream of an existence"*; *"great affection"*; *"It would, nevertheless"*; *"I shall be very unhappy"*: PC, 173, 75, 76, 76, 76–77.

27–28 *"I think you are right"*; *"When you receive"*: MC, 135–36, 136.

DISCOVERY

34–36 *"The radiation"*; *"Could we call"*; *"We propose"*; *"Gogli"*; *"roll, pick herself up"*; *"fourteen pots"*: MC, 157, 161, 161, 163, 163, 163.

36 *"a new element"*: Pierre Curie, Marie Curie, and Gustave Bémont, *On a New, Strongly Radioactive Substance, Contained in Pitchblende.* Comptes Rendus 127, 1215–17 (1898), translated and reprinted in Henry A. Boorse and Lloyd Motz, eds., *The World of the Atom,* vol. 1 (New York: Basic Books, 1966). Online source: http://web.lemoyne.edu/~giunta/curiesra.html

37–42 *"We had no money"*; *"a glass roof"*; *"had to work"*; *"We were very happy"*; *"faint, fairy lights"*; *"precious products"*; *"From all sides"*: PC, 185, 100, 101, 104, 187, 187, 104.

43 *"Ra = 225.93"*: Françoise Giroud, trans. Lydia Davis, *Marie Curie: A Life* (New York: Holmes and Meier, 1986), 101.

45 *"There is no reason"*: Ronald L. Eisenberg, M.D., *Radiology: An Illustrated History* (St. Louis: Mosby Year Book, 1992), 515.

46 *"refused to draw"*: PC, 111.

47–48 *"I have been struck"*; *"We have been doing nothing"*; *"Pierre . . . if one of us disappeared"*; *"You are wrong"*: MC, 186–87, 188, 192, 192.

48 *"The physical fatigue"*: PC, 114–15.

49 *"I had grown so accustomed"*: MC, 190.

FAME

51 *"If it is true"*: Naomi Pasachoff, *Marie Curie and the Science of Radioactivity* (New York: Oxford University Press, 1996), 55.

53 *"altogether spoiled"*: MC, 217.

53–54 *"Aren't you"* . . . *"No, you are mistaken"*; *"In science"*: MC, 220, 222.

54 *"We had become particularly attached"*: PC, 131.

TROUBLE

61 *"It has not been easy"*; *"To tell the truth"*: PC, 196, 127.

62 *"Our children"*: MC, 228.

62 *"I am neither very well"*; *"quite ill and tired"*: PC, 129, 137.

64–67 *"Pierre is dead?"*; *"On the Sunday morning"*; *"Whatever happens"*; *"I don't want a pension"*; *"When one considers"*: MC, 246, 252, 254, 252, 259.

67 *"a strange face"*: Giroud, *Marie Curie*, 146.

68 *"When Irène met strangers"*: MC, 269.

SCANDAL

71 "The method used": Marie Curie, "Radium and the New Concepts in Chemistry," Marie Curie Nobel lecture, Dec. 11, 1911. Online source: http://nobelprize.org/chemistry/laureates/1911/

72 *"So I saw at last"*: PC, 198.

73 *"women cannot be part"*: MC, 277.

73 *"Let everyone enter"*: Giroud, *Marie Curie*, 160.

74–75 *"an ambitious Pole"*; *"I am French"*: Pflaum, *Grand Obsession*, 174, 178.

75 *"Marie had been led"*: MC, 280.

78 *"I made my last pilgrimage"*: PC, 131.

WAR

82 *"I shall give you back"*: MC, 295.

85–86 *"I saw a pale"*; *"You have only"* . . . *"I? Oh, I have none"*; *"There were no patents"*: PC, 16, 17, 17.

86–88 *"What would you like"* . . . *"I need a gram"*; *"My greatest troubles"*: MC, 324, 371.

89 *"In 1906"*: PC, 191–92.

90 *"Sometimes my courage"*: MC, 373.

DANGER

95 *"exasperated and helpless"*: MC, 368.

96 *"her dentist lifted"*: Claudia Clark, *Radium Girls: Women and Industrial Health Reform, 1910–1935* (Chapel Hill: University of North Carolina Press, 1997), 34–35.

98 *"for which there was no remedy"*: The New York Times, April 28, 1928.

100 *"While other girls"*: Clark, *Radium Girls*, 212.

100–1 *"Each time there was a dangerous"* . . . *"The Curie Institute"*: Elizabeth Rona, *How It Came About: Radioactivity, Nuclear Physics, Atomic Energy* (Oak Ridge, Tenn.: Oak Ridge Associated Universities, 1978), 24, 28.

104–5 *"Mme Curie does not wish"*; *"winds lazily along"*: MC, 369, 344.

ENDINGS

110–12 *"I am worried"*; *"There was no serenity"*; *"made a point of proving"*; *"organized a motoring trip"*; *"shaken by a chill"*; *"I have a fever"*; *"Georges, look"*; *"She hardly spoke"*; *"Was it done with radium"*: MC, 376, 376, 377, 378, 378, 379, 379, 382, 383.

SELECTED BIBLIOGRAPHY

Castle, William B., M.D.; Katherine Drinker, M.D.; and Cecil K. Drinker, M.D. "Necrosis of the Jaw in Workers Employed in Applying a Luminous Paint Containing Radium." *Journal of Industrial Hygiene*. Boston: Harvard Medical School, vol. 7 (January 1925–December 1925), 371–82.

Clark, Claudia. *Radium Girls: Women and Industrial Health Reform, 1910–1935*. Chapel Hill: University of North Carolina Press, 1997.

Curie, Eve. *Madame Curie: A Biography*. Trans. by Vincent Sheean. Garden City, N.Y.: Doubleday, 1937.

Curie, Marie. *Pierre Curie*. Trans. by Charlotte and Vernon Kellogg. New York: Macmillan, 1923.

Curie, Marie. *Radioactive Substances*, a translation from the French of the classical thesis presented to the Faculty of Sciences in Paris by the distinguished Nobel Prize winner. New York: Philosophical Library, 1961.

Curie, Pierre; Marie Curie; and Gustave Bémont. *On a New, Strongly Radioactive Substance, Contained in Pitchblende*. Comptes Rendus 127, 1215–17 (1898), translated and reprinted in Henry A. Boorse and Lloyd Motz, eds., *The World of the Atom*, vol. 1 (New York: Basic Books, 1966). Online source: http://web.lemoyne.edu/~giunta/curiesra.html

Eisenberg, Ronald L., M.D. *Radiology: An Illustrated History*. St. Louis: Mosby Year Book, 1992.

"Elements That Disintegrate." The Chemistry Leaflet, Student Journal of Chemical Education. May 1, 1930.

Frame, Paul. "Natural Radioactivity in Curative Devices and Spas." *Oak Ridger*. November 5, 1989.

Frame, Paul, and William Kolb. *Living with Radiation: The First Hundred Years*, 3rd ed. Maryland: Syntec Inc., 2002.

———. "Radioactivity in Consumer Products." Oak Ridge, Tenn.: Oak Ridge Associated Universities, May 1993.

Giroud, Françoise. *Marie Curie: A Life*. Trans. by Lydia Davis. New York: Holmes and Meier, 1986.

Goldmark, Josephine. *Impatient Crusader: Florence Kelly's Life Story*. Urbana: University of Illinois Press, 1953, 189–204.

Gosling, F. G. "Dial Painters Project." *Labor's Heritage*, quarterly of the George Meany Memorial Archives, vol. 4, no. 2 (Summer 1992), 64–77.

Holcomb, William, Capt. "The World of Radiation in Everyday Life." *Radiation Safety Officer* (January/February 1999), 20–31.

Landa, Edward R. *Buried Treasure to Buried Waste: The Rise and Fall of the Radium Industry*. Colorado School of Mines, vol. 82, no. 2. Golden: Colorado School of Mines Press, 1987.

Lang, Daniel. "A Most Valuable Accident." *The New Yorker*. May 2, 1959.

Macklis, Roger, M.D. "Radithor and the Era of Mild Radium Therapy." *Journal of the American Medical Association*, vol. 264 (August 1, 1990), 614–18.

———. "The Great Radium Scandal." *Scientific American* (August 1993), 94–99.

Martin, Robert E. "Doomed to Die—and They Live!" *Popular Science*, vol. 115, no. 1 (July 1929), 17–19, 156.

Martland, Harrison S., M.D. "The Occurrence of Malignancy in Radioactive Persons: A General Review of Data Gathered in the Study of the Radium Dial Painters, with Special Reference to the Occurrence of Osteogenic Sarcoma and the Inter-relationship of Certain Blood Diseases." *American Journal of Cancer*, vol. 15, no. 4 (October 1931), 112–19.

Martland, Harrison S., M.D., and Robert E. Humphries, M.D. *Osteogenic Sarcoma in*

Dial Painters Using Luminous Paint. Read before the New York Pathological Society at the New York Academy of Medicine, March 8, 1928.

McCoy, Bob. *Quack! Tales of Medical Fraud from the Museum of Questionable Medical Devices.* Santa Monica, Calif.: Santa Monica Press, 2000, 95–114.

McGrayne, Sharon Betsch. *Nobel Prize Women in Science: Their Lives, Struggles, and Momentous Discoveries.* New York: Birch Lane Press, 1993, 11–36.

Milne, Lorus J., and Margery Milne. *Understanding Radioactivity.* New York: Atheneum, 1989.

Mok, Michael. "Radium: Life-giving Element Deals Death in the Hands of Quacks." *Popular Science*, vol. 121, no. 1 (July 1932), 9–10, 105–6.

Mould, Richard F. *A Century of X-Rays and Radioactivity in Medicine With Emphasis on Photographic Records of the Early Years.* Philadelphia: Institute of Physics Publishing, 1993.

———. *Mould's Medical Anecdotes,* Omnibus Edition. Philadelphia: Institute of Physics Publishing, 1996, 421–28.

Neuzil, Mark. *Mass Media and Environmental Conflict: America's Green Crusades.* Thousand Oaks, Calif.: Sage Publications, 1996: 33–52.

Pasachoff, Naomi. *Marie Curie and the Science of Radioactivity.* New York: Oxford University Press, 1996.

Pflaum, Rosalynd. *Grand Obsession: Marie Curie and Her World.* New York: Doubleday, 1989.

Quinn, Susan. *Marie Curie: A Life.* New York: Simon and Schuster, 1995.

Rona, Elizabeth. *How It Came About: Radioactivity, Nuclear Physics, Atomic Energy.* Oak Ridge, Tenn.: Oak Ridge Associated Universities, 1978.

Schubert, Jack, and Ralph E. Lapp. *Radiation: What It Is and How It Affects You.* New York: Viking, 1957.

RECOMMENDED WEB SITES

http://www.orau.org/ptp/museumdirectory.htm

Dr. Paul Frame maintains the Web site of the Health Physics Historical Instrumentation Museum Collection for Oak Ridge Associated Universities. This museum is dedicated to preserving the scientific and commercial history of radioactivity and radiation. You can learn more about some of the images in this book plus hundreds more by visiting this fascinating site.

http://www.curie.fr/fondation/musee/index.cfm/lang/_gb.htm

This is the official Web site for the Curie Museum, housed in Marie Curie's Radium Institute.

http://www.iem-inc.com/

A Web site provided by Integrated Environmental Management, Inc., that provides a great deal of information on radiation.

http://science.howstuffworks.com/nuclear.htm

A wonderful Web site that explains how many different things work, including nuclear radiation, nuclear bombs, radon, carbon-14 dating, and X-rays.

http://pearl1.lanl.gov/periodic/default.htm

The Los Alamos National Laboratory's Chemistry Division has created this site for students to learn more about the periodic table of the elements, which was originated by Dmitri Mendeleev.

http://www.nei.org/scienceclub/nuclearworld.html

An animated Web site by the Nuclear Energy Institute that covers the subject of nuclear energy.

http://www.nobel.se

This is Sweden's Nobel "e-Museum," where visitors can access Pierre and Marie's Nobel lectures, among other information.

ACKNOWLEDGMENTS

My deepest appreciation goes to Dr. Paul Frame for reviewing this manuscript and for sharing information, photographs, and research material with me. His expertise has been invaluable.

Many thanks to Lenka Brochard at the Association Curie et Joliot-Curie, who allowed me to look through photographs of the Curie family and provided many of the images seen in these pages. I will always remember her kindness to me when I visited Paris. *Merci beaucoup*, Madame Brochard.

I'd also like to thank the staff at the Curie Museum in Paris, especially Nathalie Huchette, a gracious tour guide, who allowed me to sit at Marie Curie's desk.

My gratitude goes to Radiology Centennial, Inc., the American College of Radiology, and Jim Morrison for allowing me to use their images.

I'd like to thank Lois Densky-Wolff at the University of Medicine and Dentistry of New Jersey for providing me with photographs of the Radium Girls.

My appreciation also goes to Robbie Mayes, my editor at Farrar, Straus and Giroux, for his precise and insightful editing, and to Elaine Chubb and Selma Rayfiel for their attention to detail. Each of them helped make this the book I knew it could be.

ILLUSTRATION CREDITS

Permission to reprint many of the images in this book has been provided by the Association Curie et Joliot-Curie. These pictures include the dust jacket image and the frontispiece, as well as those appearing on the following pages: 6, 8, 18, 21, 29, 33, 35, 37, 43, 53, 76, 77, 81, 83, 87, 88, 102, 104, and 111.

Permission to reprint the images on pages 45, 56, 84, 92, 93, and 97 has been generously provided by the American College of Radiology through Radiology Centennial, Inc.

Photographs courtesy of the Oak Ridge Associated Universities are to be found on pages 46, 57, 58, 69, 85, 94, 96, 101, 105, 106, 108, and 109.

The photographs on pages 98 and 99 are courtesy of the University of Medicine and Dentistry of New Jersey Libraries, Special Collections, Harrison S. Martland Papers.

Finally, the photograph of the Radium Institute on page 78 appears courtesy of the author.

INDEX